MAKE YOUR OWN BUCKET LIST

How to Design Yours Before You Kick It

Andrew Gall
Design by Matt Webb

adamsmedia
AVON, MASSACHUSETTS

Acknowledgments

Andrew

For my wife and parents. And anyone inspired to do fun, different, interesting things every day.

Matt

For my family and my two favorite girls, Jenny and Lucy. You inspire me to lead as interesting a life as possible.

Published by
Adams Media, a division of F+W Media, Inc.
57 Littlefield Street, Avon, MA 02322. U.S.A.
www.adamsmedia.com

ISBN 13: 978-1-4351-5883-2

Printed in the United States of America.

10 9 8 7 6 5 4 3 2 1

Introduction

You're not dead yet. Let us rejoice and be glad.

If you're reading this, have we got some good news for you: you're alive. Congratulations! Why, on today of all days, should the fact that you're alive be such a great revelation? Well, other than general rejoicing about being a living, breathing object at this moment, thanks to this book, you've got a lot of meaningful living left to do.

Many bucket lists dictate things you should do or see before you die. Climb a mountain. See *Cats*. Bring cats to see *Cats*. We, on the other hand, know that every human being is different. Each is a unique, curious being. That's why we've created this book: a bucket list generator. Contained herein, you'll find a couple hundred pages filled with rough categories and prompts that will get you to the answers *you* can decide upon, rather than have them dictated to you, like in the case of some old dictationist person who works for a CEO who wears ill-fitting slacks.

So, why not get started? There's lots of living left to be lived.

Again, kudos on the whole being alive thing. You're very fortunate. And you look great, too.

BUCKET LIST ENTRY #1

CONFRONT A PAST EMBARRASSMENT

1. Think about the most embarrassing thing you've ever done.

   Was it nudity related? Indoors or outdoors? Did it involve the losing of pants?
   Go ahead, spill the beans.

   ____

   ____

   ____

2. The only thing that could have been more embarrassing than what you did would be: (check one)

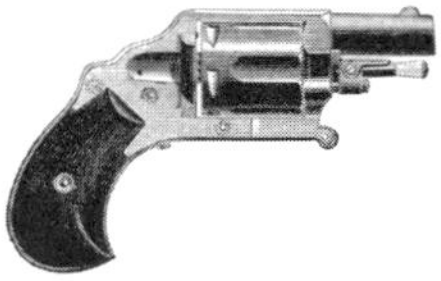

- ☐ *accidentally and singlehandedly sinking your uncle's sailboat*
- ☐ *pronouncing "Russian roulette" as if it were "Russian rou-lay"*
- ☐ *slipping on a banana peel (cliché, but really could happen)*

3. Could you re-create the embarrassing scenario in a different city (or even better, a different *country*) in front of a large group of strangers? If so, do that.

IF NOT

Find a way to get the attention of a crowd at a major sporting event, parade, or other public gathering.

BUCKET LIST ENTRY #1

STARE AN EMBARRASSING MOMENT IN THE FACE AND WIN BY:

BUCKET LIST ENTRY #2

Eat the Most Memorable Meal Imaginable

1. What is your favorite food?

2. Write down, in one word, the way you feel after eating your favorite food.

3. If you had to describe what it feels like to taste your favorite food, it would be most like: (check one)

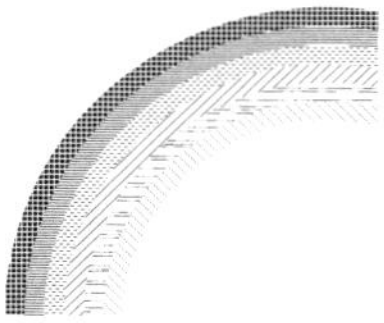

☐ *a rainbow* ☐ *going for a moonlight swim* ☐ *a musk that smells like birch wood* ☐ *swing sets*

4. Do you know where your favorite dish/meal was invented? Was it a field in the small town of Chesterton? A famous sidewalk café? An uncle's garage? Get as specific as possible. And if you don't know, go look it up. We'll wait.

____

____

____

____

____

____

5. Enjoy your favorite dish in the best possible way: in the place it was created. If it's salmon, go eat it in Seattle. If it's pizza, pack your bags for Italy.

BUCKET LIST ENTRY # 2

MAKE YOUR STOMACH THANK YOU A MILLION TIMES BY ENJOYING AN UNFORGETTABLE MEAL OF

____

IN ____ .

BUCKET LIST ENTRY #3

Embark Upon an Epic Animal Adventure

1. What is your favorite nondomesticated animal (that is, your favorite animal excluding a dog or cat)?[1,2]

2. Why do you love this animal so much?

[1]Wild dogs okay, jungle cats okay, Persian cats *not* okay.

[2]It does not have to be your technical spirit animal, though you may think of it this way if it will help you.

3. Draw your favorite nondomesticated animal below from memory to exemplify your true passion for your favorite nondomesticated animal.

YOUR ANIMAL

4. Where is this animal most commonly found?

5. Have you ever seen this animal in this place before?

- ☐ *Yes*
- ☐ *No*

IF NOT

Visit your animal in its natural habitat by trekking, safari-ing, swimming with, or otherwise observing it.

IF SO

What is your second favorite animal? Third favorite? Repeat steps above until you come to one you haven't seen in its natural habitat. No matter what, you'll wind up seeing someplace new.

BUCKET LIST ENTRY #3

I'M GOING TO SATISFY MY ANIMAL URGE BY:

BUCKET LIST ENTRY #4

Write the Best Thing You've Ever Written

1. I've always wanted to write: (check one)

   - ☐ *an article*
   - ☐ *a short story*
   - ☐ *a short story about short stories*
   - ☐ *a novel*
   - ☐ *something else literarily fantastic*

2. How much time are you willing to commit to making it happen? Years? Months? Days? Hours? Put down a number and commit to it.

BUCKET LIST ENTRY #4

I'M GOING TO REALIZE MY BOOKISH FANTASY BY: (DESCRIBE WHAT YOU'RE GOING TO WRITE BY WRITING IT HERE)

____

____

____

____

____

BUCKET LIST ENTRY #5

Conquer Your Biggest Fear

1. What is your single-most frightening, painful, or otherwise palm-sweat-inducing memory?

2. Identify the exact cause of the fear. Is it a who? A what? A where?

3. Why do you think you're so afraid?

4. Is it scarier than this?

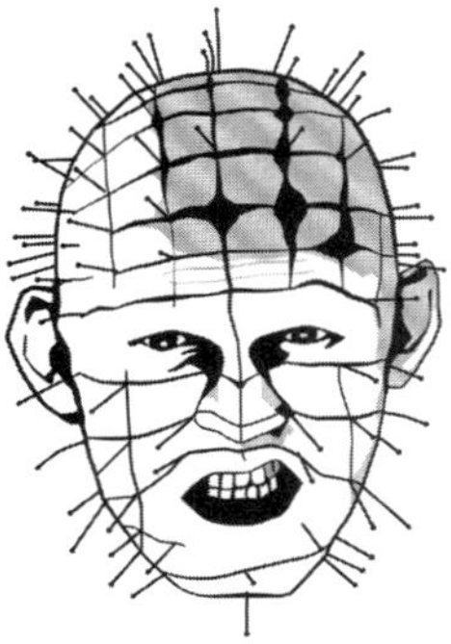

☐ *Yes* ☐ *No*

☐ *Yes* ☐ *No*

5. It's time to face your fear head on—and more importantly, conquer it. Decide how you'll do it below.

BUCKET LIST ENTRY #5

I WILL CONFRONT, DEAL WITH, OR RELIVE THE ONE PERSON, PLACE, THING, OR EVENT I'M MOST AFRAID OF BY:

BUCKET LIST ENTRY #6

Live Out Your Favorite Scene from Your Favorite Movie

1. What is your all-time favorite movie?

2. In your favorite movie, which scene do you find to be most memorable?

3. Where is the scene set?

4. Have you ever acted out the scene:

- ☐ *at home when no one else is around?*
- ☐ *for someone else?*
- ☐ *in front of a hot dog cart?*[1]

5. Is it a real place? Notre Dame Stadium, where they carried Rudy off the field? Chinatown? Gotham City? If so, go there.

IF NOT

Do the next best thing and improvise. If it's Tatooine from *Star Wars*, find out which real desert they used. If it's the balloon-propelled house from *Up*, find the real-life house that inspired it. Get creative.

BUCKET LIST ENTRY #6

I WILL REENACT MY FAVORITE MOVIE SCENE BY:

[1] Irrelevant if your favorite scene already involves a hot dog cart.

BUCKET LIST ENTRY #7

Drive Cross-Country

1. Where will you start?

2. Where will you end?

3. Use the sample routes below for inspiration.

4. Now draw the route you want to take.

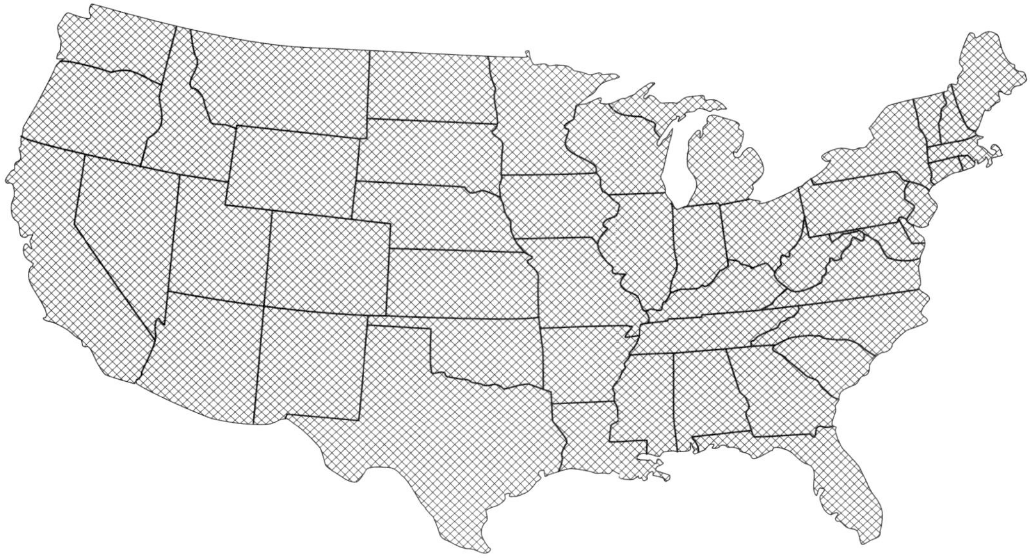

BUCKET LIST ENTRY #7

I WILL DRIVE CROSS-COUNTRY ANY WAY I CHOOSE AND VISIT THE FOLLOWING STATES:

BUCKET LIST ENTRY #8

Invent Something

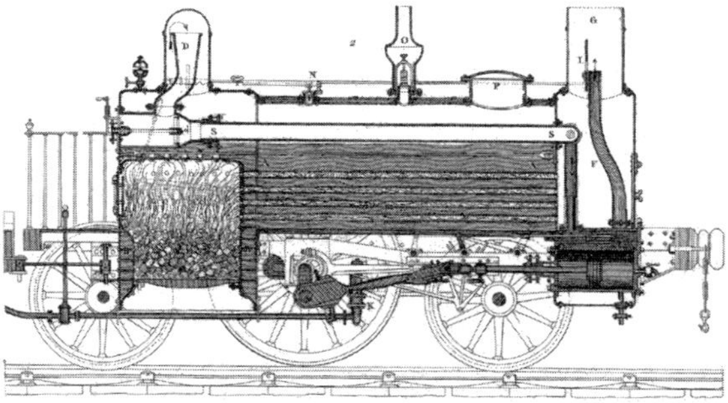

1. Everyone has some sort of weird special fascination. Sports. Science. Sidecars. What's yours?

2. Is there something you can think of that can make that fascination easier, better, or . . . more fascinating?

3. Your ideal invention would be made mostly of:

- ☐ *wood*
- ☐ *rubber*
- ☐ *wood made of rubber*
- ☐ *acrylic*
- ☐ *ball bearings, because it's all ball bearings these days*
- ☐ *other*

4. Do you know a patent lawyer?

- ☐ *Yes*
- ☐ *No*

5. If so, does he/she look like this?

☐ *Yes* ☐ *No*

6. If you do know a patent lawyer, contact one and see if he or she can do research for you. If not, see if you can somehow get in touch with one. If that's still not possible, start mapping out your invention any way you can—on a napkin, on a sketchpad, on an official blueprint.

7. Next, spend some time on Google for a bit. Does a similar invention already exist? If so, start over. If not, refine your design and go forward. Even if your idea for an invention never becomes an actual physical device that allows dogs to more easily eat Snausages, you could still wind up with the next great idea.

BUCKET LIST ENTRY #8

THE INVENTION I WOULD INVENT WOULD BE A:

____

____

____

____

____

____

BUCKET LIST ENTRY #9

Do Your Dream Job for the Day

1. Is your dream job to be a baseball umpire?

    ☐ *Yes*
    ☐ *No*

    This question is irrelevant, as being a baseball umpire is, of course, secretly *everyone's* dream job.

2. What is your dream job?

    ____

    ____

    ____

3. Do you know anyone who actually holds your dream job? If so, shadow him or her for a day and live out what it's like.

4. If you don't, or that's just not possible, pursue the next best thing. Befriend someone who does it and spend time with that person. And if you can't do *that*, try something else. If your dream is to be president of the United States, pontificate wildly and set up a bunch of meetings. If it's professional basketball, go to a fantasy camp.

BUCKET LIST ENTRY #9

I'M GOING TO LIVE OUT MY DREAM OCCUPATION BY:

BUCKET LIST ENTRY #10

Find a Charitable Cause and Make a Meaningful Contribution

1. Do you have an easily identifiable passion? An animal? A political cause? A policy? A sport?

2. You definitely do, even if you don't know it. Think harder. What do you think about? Read about? What stirs you?

3. Okay, thought so. Now, think about that passion. What do you know about it? Do some research to learn what kind of charitable causes or activities are out there. Like a bear deciding which fish to eat for dinner, it's always best to know your options.

4. What's the best way you can contribute to this cause? If it's sports, teach sports to kids. If it's an animal, give monetarily or build awareness. If it's helping others, join the Red Cross for the year.

BUCKET LIST ENTRY #10

I'm going to give generously by:

BUCKET LIST ENTRY #11

Push Yourself to the Limit of Your Favorite Physical Activity

1. What is your favorite physical activity?[1]

[1] "Slothing" is not an acceptable answer.

2. Describe your history and/or proudest accomplishments related to said activity.

3. Do you have any cool trophies? Describe them.

4. What could you do in regard to said activity that you've never done? Do that.

BUCKET LIST ENTRY #11

I'm going to make the endorphins flow freely by:

BUCKET LIST ENTRY #12

Experience Your Ultimate Water Adventure

1. How beautiful do you find water?

   a. *Picturesque*
   b. *The most beautifullest thing in this world*
   c. *Like a pearl in the ocean . . . in the ocean*

2. Have you ever owned a slip-and-slide?

   ☐ *Yes*
   ☐ *No*
   ☐ *I hate my parents :,(*

3. Are you a pirate?[1]

   ☐ *Yes*
   ☐ *No*

4. What do you like most about water?[2]

   ____

   ____

   ____

[1] If you answered yes, you have already had your ultimate water adventure. Well done, Scallywag.

[2] If your answer is something completely water averse, like "Just thinking about swimming in open water causes me to scissor-kick my legs in protest," do something that has water involved but on land. Take the most amazing shower. Rent a Jacuzzi. Sing in the rain. Watch *Jaws*. You're done here. Just write your answer at the end and ignore the next query.

5. Assuming you do, in fact, like water, research what you can do to make what you love most about being on the water the biggest aquatic occurrence of your lifetime. If you love boating, make your way onto a yacht, or take a once-in-a-lifetime cruise. If you love diving, swim with the dolphins. Use your imagination and see what happens.

BUCKET LIST ENTRY #12

I WILL VISIT MY OWN PERSONAL AQUATIC SHANGRI-LA BY:

BUCKET LIST ENTRY #13

Experience What It's Like to Live During Your Favorite Time Period

1. What's your favorite time period (other than the one you're in right now) that you wish you could live in?

2. Circle the character that best defines your favorite time period:

3. What's the most famous physical location for your favorite time period? A speakeasy? The corner of Haight and Ashbury during the sixties? Find out and visit it. If that's not possible, find out if it's possible to somehow reenact that time period via tour, festival, or renaissance faire. Immerse yourself, particularly if it involves a renaissance faire. (And get the apples on a stick while you're at it.)

BUCKET LIST ENTRY #13

I'M CHOOSING TO GET DOWN WITH MY FAVORITE HISTORICAL TIME PERIOD BY:

BUCKET LIST ENTRY #14

Learn to Do That Thing You've Always Wanted to Learn to Do

1. What is the one thing you've always wanted to learn to do?

   a. *Unicycling*
   b. *Other*______________________________________

2. How do you think that you do that thing you've always wanted to learn to do?

   a. *Pedal and have good balance*
   b. ______________________________________

3. Look it up. Were you right? If so, read about how to do it and then do it. If not, same thing. Can you take lessons? Have a friend teach you? Or is this a journey to the center of your newfound earth you want to take your own self? Sounds good, journey taker.

BUCKET LIST ENTRY #14

Paste a photo of yourself doing that new thing here, replacing this excellent drawing of a man acting out the act of pedaling a recumbent bike without an actual recumbent bike (that is, air-recumbence).

BUCKET LIST ENTRY #15

Wear Something That Would Normally Embarrass You in Public

1. Like it or not, everyone is fashionable in their own way. Even lack of fashion is a fashion. Profound, we know.

2. Define your fashion sense in one word.

   ☐ *"Trendy"*
   ☐ *"Superfly"*
   ☐ *"Mrrrraaahhhh"*

3. List your favorite items of clothing to wear. List as many as you want!

   ____
   ____
   ____

4. Now list your least favorite items.

5. How could you make these least favorite items even worse? For example, if you hate wearing scarves, could you wear a scarf that's neon? If you hate hats, could you wear a top hat? If you hate pants, could you wear hot pants?

6. Now it's time to unleash your out-of-the-ordinary fashions on the world. Settle on something and wear it for a day in public. Get as much exposure as possible. Show it off. Enjoy the reactions, knowing that you will never wear whatever godforsaken thing it is again. Take pictures!

BUCKET LIST ENTRY #15

I'M GOING TO KNOWINGLY CREATE MY BIGGEST FASHION FAUX PAS EVER BY:

BUCKET LIST ENTRY #16

Learn How to Defend Yourself

1. If this came upon you in the wild, how would you defend yourself?

2. And this?

3. What if *this* came upon you, and you were at home?

4. And how about this, only this time you're at home and not even wearing socks?

5. Do you know how to defend yourself? What's your go-to technique?

6. What aspect of self-defense sounds most interesting to you? Learning how to shoot a gun? Getting a tae kwon do black belt? Learning to box? Simply studying the most painful pressure points on the human body? Pick an answer and try it out. Take a class. Do some research. Then, if you don't like it, walk away. Start over if you want, but remember that knowing how to defend yourself is an extremely valuable skill. No matter how genial, nonconfrontational, or downright mayoral you may seem.

BUCKET LIST ENTRY #16

I'm going to learn how to make bullies cry (even if I never have to actually make bullies cry) by:

BUCKET LIST ENTRY #17

Make a Summer Reading List

1. Make next summer the literary tour de force you've always wanted to tour the force of. Write down at least seven books that you'll commit to reading.

2. Find all kinds of places to enjoy a book in the (presumed) nice weather—your deck, under a tree, on your uncle's boat. And let the words soak into your head just like the sun you're currently also in the process of soaking in. And remember, don't burn. Words sound much harsher when you burn.

BUCKET LIST ENTRY #17

NEXT SUMMER, HERE'S WHAT I'M READING:

BUCKET LIST ENTRY #18

Visit a Place Wholly and Totally Out of Your Element

1. What is your element? A city? A state? A town? A specific warm couch?

2. What do you think would be totally opposite of that element?

3. Is it a physical location or a theoretical one (e.g., a place where people have fish for heads)?

____

____

____

____

____

4. If it's a physical location, go there for at least five days (if it's a new country, town, or city, take a trip). If it's more of a specific place like Red Square on the University of Washington college campus, go there every day for a week or for five weekends in a row. You get the idea. In other words, long enough until you feel comfortable shaking the hand of that omnipresent dreadlocked man. Wherever it is, go there and gain a new perspective.

BUCKET LIST ENTRY #18

I'M GOING TO GO TO ____________________ FOR ____*amount of time*____,

SOMEWHERE THAT FEELS AS OUT OF MY ELEMENT AS WEARING WOMEN'S PANTS IF I WERE A MAN. OR MEN'S PANTS IF I WERE A WOMAN.

BUCKET LIST ENTRY #19

Live Out Your Dream Music Experience

1. What's your favorite thing about music?

   - ☐ *Going to live music shows of my favorite artist*
   - ☐ *Going to music festivals and seeing all kinds of different artists or multiple favorite artists (you don't have to enjoy portable toilets filled with toilet detritus to pick this option)*
   - ☐ *Staying at home and listening to music*

2. Think about your favorite music experience up until now. Was it listening to a certain album for the first time? A certain show? A certain festival? Describe the depths and breadths of all your sonic love.

3. Think about how amazing this picture is, then think about whether your experience was more amazing.

4. Think back to what you picked for Question 1. Now think of how you could do whatever answer you picked on as big a scale as possible and do it. If your answer was a, go see that artist where they have the biggest following, or a famous venue, or somewhere amazing you've never been to. Same thing for b: see the biggest music fest ever. If it's c, get creative and turn your home into some special sonic world—buy a new stereo, have Kravitzfest, whatever.

BUCKET LIST ENTRY #19

I'M READY TO ENJOY MUSICAL BOOMTOWN BY:

____

____

____

____

____

BUCKET LIST ENTRY #20

Share One Unique Talent You Have with the World

1. Think of something unique to yourself that you happen to be good at and write it here. It can be physical, mental, even something you think you're good at but would like to pursue further (e.g., dog sledding).

____

____

____

2. Do you think you could get even better at this? Seriously. If you think you could get better, do that first by practicing, then proceed.

☐ *Yes*
☐ *No*

3. Do people know that you're good at this?

☐ *Yes*
☐ *No*

4. Does Arsenio Hall know that you're good at this?

   - ☐ *Yes*
   - ☐ *No*

5. Accomplish what you want to accomplish and share this talent with as many people as you can. Write a book and get it published; do seventy-eight one-handed pushups and post it to YouTube. Send the tape of you armpit farting a Maya Angelou poem to your local news outlet. Whatever it is, *the world must see it.*

BUCKET LIST ENTRY #20

I'M GOING TO SHOW THE WORLD I'VE GOT TALENT BY:

BUCKET LIST ENTRY #21

See the Most Amazing Natural Wonder Your Eyes Have Ever Wondered Upon

1. Familiarize yourself with the natural wonders of the world (via Internet, memory, or asking that nearby guy in the large foam ten-gallon hat).

2. Which one of them looks the most interesting to you?

3. If none looks interesting, which has the coolest name?

4. If still none, which one rhymes with "Prone Wenge"?

5. Go to whichever answers the above best.

BUCKET LIST ENTRY #21

I'M GOING TO SEE THE MOST WONDERFUL NATURAL WONDER IN THE HISTORY OF WONDROUSNESS BY VISITING:

BUCKET LIST ENTRY #22

Get Crafty

1. What's the best artistic or crafty construction your talented hands have ever produced?

2. Is there anything crafty you immediately feel like you'd want to learn? If so, get started by taking a local class or buying the materials and doing a little self-experimenting.

   - ☐ *Yes*
   - ☐ *No*

3. If you answered no, it doesn't mean you are unimaginative, hopeless, or have fat, meaty hands. It just means you have to look inward a little more inwardly. Think a little harder. Quilting? Crocheting? Scrapbooking? Putting your digital photos into a photo book? Calligraphy? Any of these ringing any potential fun bells? Just pick something. Throw darts at a craft-themed dartboard if you have to. It may be better this way, as you could wind up acquiring an interest you never in this great nation thought you would ever have.

BUCKET LIST ENTRY #22

I'M GOING TO FIND MY INNER CRAFTSPERSON BY LEARNING HOW TO:

____

AND MAKING ______________________________________.

BUCKET LIST ENTRY #23

Visit a World-Class Art Museum

1. What kind of art do you like the most?[1]

[1] "Nothing specific" or "I don't really have an interest in art" are both acceptable answers, and no one will peer down upon you with horn-rimmed glasses for writing either of these.

2. If there is a specific kind of art you like, you should go see what you like most in the most interesting and memorable place possible. MOMA in New York, or the Louvre in Paris, for example. Now, we know art is subjective, so you're going to have to use a bit of your imagination on this one. So make a choice.

3. If you're less of an art connoisseur, don't fret, as you should still go see some art. Maybe this will help stoke the flame of a new and different love that you haven't previously loved before. So here's to your new art love: Just pick a museum that looks interesting and go there. Your ultimate art experience can always be one-upped—that's the beauty of living, Mr. or Mrs. Human.

BUCKET LIST ENTRY #23

I AM GOING TO GO SEE ____*name a specific museum, exhibit, or type of art*____

IN ____.

BUCKET LIST ENTRY #24

Go to the Coolest Cultural Festival Ever

1. Write down your favorite culture, other than your own. If you hate your own culture, that's fine, too.

____

____

____

2. Describe what you like the most about that culture.

____

____

____

3. Identify, from these photos, which one of these is, in fact, lederhosen.

4. Now that you've decided your favorite culture and identified lederhosen correctly (we assume), get to know that culture a bit. What traditions do they have that sound so awesome they make sprouting a second head seem entirely possible?

____

____

____

5. Now see if there is a festival celebrating these traditions. If so, go to that festival—in the native country, if possible. If not, do the next best thing: Do a local version (Oktoberfest, for example). Wear the costumes. Dance the dances. Eat the delicacies that may or may not be chocolate-covered grasshoppers. Live it up.

BUCKET LIST ENTRY #24

I'M GOING TO EXPLORE CULTURAL COOLNESS BY:

____

____

____

____

____

BUCKET LIST ENTRY #25

Decide Who You'd Most Want to Meet Before You Die and Do It

1. List five living famous people you admire.

2. What is it about them that you admire? List at least three traits per famous person.

3. Are all of them people you would like to meet? Or are any of them people you are fine with admiring from afar, like a gentle and rare animal (e.g., an aardwolf).

4. Of the famous people you would like to meet, which one would you most like to meet?

5. Do you think it's possible? Assuming you're a positive person that is resourceful and committed to meeting this person, make it happen. If you don't think it's possible, choose another from your list.

BUCKET LIST ENTRY #25

I'M GOING TO CHANNEL MY ADMIRATION OF SOMEONE INTO ACTUALLY MEETING THAT SOMEONE BY:

BUCKET LIST ENTRY #26

Start and Maintain a Collection of Something

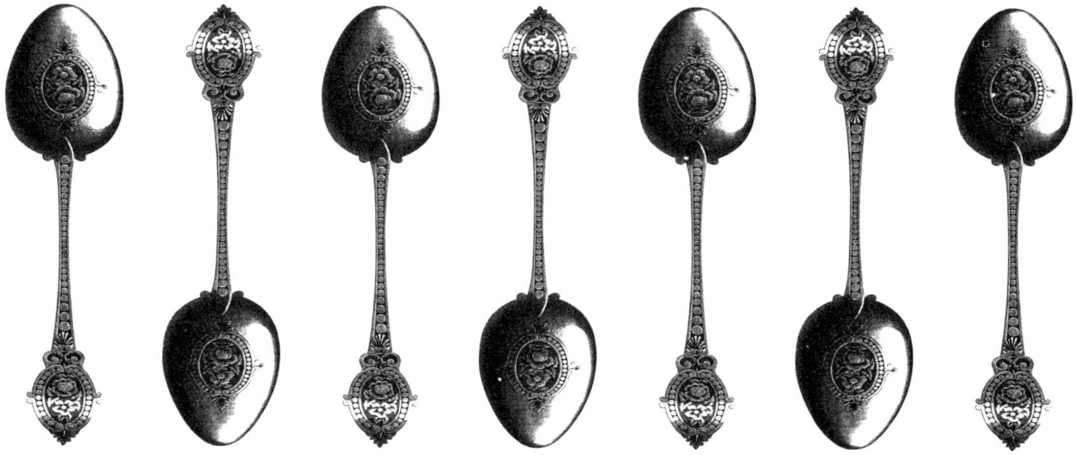

1. What did you collect growing up?

____

____

____

____

____

2. Your reasons for collecting were: (check all that apply)

   - ☐ *fun*
   - ☐ *potential monetary gain*
   - ☐ *social collecting*
   - ☐ *parents made me*
   - ☐ *parents' friends made me*
   - ☐ *because I am a hoarder*
   - ☐ *because of Winn-Dixie*

3. Do you already have a collection of something? If so, and if you don't want to start a new one, rediscover it. Grow it. Learn the most you can about it. Most importantly, maintain and take a renewed pride in having it.

   If not, start one. It can be any object, doohickey, dawdle, meep, or schmoo. Well, not any schmoo. Just pick something fun and start collecting. And remember, it's only hoarding if you forget what color your carpet is.

BUCKET LIST ENTRY #26

I'M GOING TO START / MAINTAIN / GROW A COLLECTION OF:

BUCKET LIST ENTRY #27

Become Especially Well Read in Something

1. Write down a specific person, place, thing, or author that especially intrigues or interests you.

____

____

____

2. Which author below seems to be the most intriguing?

3. Consider the subject matter. Could you read every single book ever written in that genre or by that author? List as many as you can find here, then attack them with your eyes and brain vociferously, one by one.

4. Does your passion burn even further? If so, use this space to write down articles, movies, abstracts, dissertations, laser disc contents, and anything else about said subject you want to delve in to, then delve into it. Happy experting!

BUCKET LIST ENTRY #27

I'M GOING TO BECOME RIDICULOUSLY WELL READ IN THE REALM OF

BY READING OR OTHERWISE CONSUMING EVERYTHING LISTED ABOVE.

BUCKET LIST ENTRY #28

Become a Star at Something (Or at Least Audition to Show the World What You've Got)

1. Everyone should audition for a role in something at least once in their life. If you had the talent, what would you want that to be?

2. Do you know anyone who could help prepare you for this? If not, how about a friend of a friend? Do some searching until you find someone who can help you—this person will have any combination of the right knowledge, the right experience, and the right connections.

3. To be properly prepared for fame, you must choose your muse (paparazzi, on-camera interviewers, people on the street, and Billy Bush will all want to know this answer once you become famous).

4. Find a way to try out for a role. If you want to sing, try to audition for *American Idol* or another reality show, or keep it local if you want. If it's theater or acting, audition for a community theater role. Just get out there. After all, they just might like you. Really, really like you.

BUCKET LIST ENTRY #28

I'M GOING TO AUDITION FOR A ROLE OF ______________________________

BY SEEKING OUT AN AUDITION IN ______________________________ .

BUCKET LIST ENTRY #29

Accomplish Something Musically

1. Can you play "Stairway to Heaven" on your guitar?

   ☐ *Yes*
   ☐ *No*

2. Don't.

3. Describe what you'd most like to accomplish musically.

4. Pick a part of the music world you'd most like to immerse yourself in. Compose a song on a guitar. Make a beat for a hip-hop track. Write and sing one song—and get it professionally produced by booking studio time. Perform a song you like or a song you've made for someone. Whatever it is, use this "rock on" symbol below to inspire you.

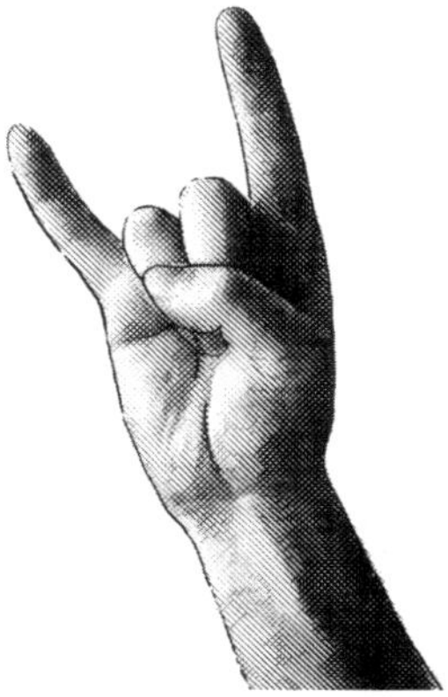

BUCKET LIST ENTRY #29

I'M GOING TO BECOME ACCOMPLISHED MUSICALLY—BY ACCOMPLISHING SOMETHING MUSICALLY. THAT THING I WILL ACCOMPLISH MUSICALLY WILL BE:

____

____

____

____

____

BUCKET LIST ENTRY #30

Learn a Foreign Language

1. Which foreign languages do you know? Do you know any quite well, or at least quite intermittently? Describe your foreign language skills below.

____

____

____

____

2. Which language would you most want to learn?[1]

____

____

____

____

[1] This doesn't have to be a "foreign language" in the traditional sense. There's nothing wrong with wanting to become fluent in Klingon or whatever language that one guy in *Fat Albert* speaks. Just identify one below. No judgments here.

3. If you already know a language quite well, how can you push it further? What else can you learn to become even more proficient?

4. If you know next to nothing, sign up for a class, or at least buy some books. Set aside and commit to a learning cycle. And once you're ready, go speak it.

BUCKET LIST ENTRY #30

I WILL BECOME WELL SPOKEN IN A WHOLE NEW DIALECT BY LEARNING OR CONTINUING TO MASTER

____

VIA *tell us how you plan to master it and what you're committing to, timewise, to do so* .

BUCKET LIST ENTRY #31

Confront Your Fear of Stage Fright

1. What is the one thing you'd be the most afraid to do in front of an audience?

____

____

____

2. Why do you think it makes you so afraid or intimidated?

____

____

____

3. Circle the number on the number line to rate how likely it would be that you would pee your pants. (With 100 being the most likely for pee to occur.)

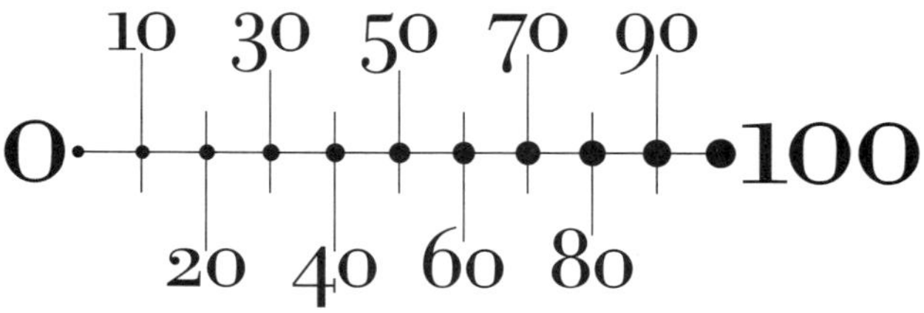

4. Put your pee prediction to the test. Whatever you wrote down to answer Question 1, do it. Give a presentation. Write and perform a comedy routine in a local bar. Sing a song. Read a poem on poetry night. Whatever it is, seek out an audience and make it happen.

BUCKET LIST ENTRY #31

I'm going to perform for an audience (and, hopefully, not pee my pants) by:

BUCKET LIST ENTRY #32

Have Some Fun in the Sky

1. Describe something interesting you've done while being skyward.

2. Have you ever found yourself face to face with a bird?

☐ *Yes*
☐ *No*

3. Would you say you are afraid of the sky? Or would you consider the sky to be a friend—the kind of friend whom you would let borrow your bicycle without even having to ask?

☐ *Afraid*
☐ *Not afraid*

4. Is it possible for you to overcome your fear of the sky? If so, proceed. If not, that's okay. Instead, think of a fun skyward fantasy you'd undertake and write a story about that. If you can't live it, you can at least imagine it.

5. What's one thing, sky-related, that you've always wanted to try? Try it. It could be anything from a hot-air balloon ride to skydiving to just flying first class. Whatever it is, just get out there. Up there, rather.

BUCKET LIST ENTRY #32

I'M GOING TO MAKE THE MOST OF THE FRIENDLY SKIES BY:

____

____

____

____

____

BUCKET LIST ENTRY #33

Do One Thing Completely Out of Your Societal Comfort Zone

1. No one likes the Upper Crust. But if there's one thing they do that you've always dreamed of doing, what would it be?[1]

2. If you can't think of anything, take it down a notch. Maybe you don't want to try caviar or drive a Ferrari, but maybe you'd enjoy spending the night in a castle. Or fly first class. Whatever it is, only you know if it's something truly out of your element. And you should do it at least once. But if you start wearing a monocle or saying "tut-tut" in casual conversation, that's when you'll know you've gone too far.

BUCKET LIST ENTRY #33

I am going to live as the 1 percent lives, at least for a fleeting moment, by:

[1] *Important note*: If you are part of the 1 percent, hello. Thank you for giving Lamborghinis a reason to live.

BUCKET LIST ENTRY #34

Design Your Dream Something

1. Check off one of these:

   - ☐ *dream house*
   - ☐ *dream office*
   - ☐ *dream getaway*
   - ☐ *dream ice cream sundae*
   - ☐ *dream pillowcase*
   - ☐ *dream bedroom*
   - ☐ *dream kitchen*
   - ☐ *dream basement*
   - ☐ *dream garage*
   - ☐ *dream shower*
   - ☐ *dream garden*
   - ☐ *dream chili parlor that you own and also work the counter*

2. Make it happen.

BUCKET LIST ENTRY #34

I WILL DESIGN MY DREAM SOMETHING AND MAKE IT A REAL SOMETHING BY:

BUCKET LIST ENTRY #35

Visit a Kick-Ass Theme Park

1. People don't give theme parks enough credit. What is your favorite theme park?

2. How many times have you been there?

3. If the answer is zero times, go there. Also, how could it be your favorite theme park if you have never been to it? It's so confusing!

4. If you don't have a favorite theme park, expand the definition of "theme park" a little bit to fit your needs. It could be a baseball stadium. Or a concert venue. It doesn't have to feature plastic mouse ears and meat on a stick (though that would be nice, speaking generally). If you have one theme park you've already been to, can you go to a better version of that? Disney World versus Disneyland, for example? Or if not, go again. But this time, stay longer. Do more. Bring a friend. And more snacks.

BUCKET LIST ENTRY #35

I'M GOING TO HAVE MY BEST THEME PARK EXPERIENCE IN THE HISTORY OF THEME PARK EXPERIENCES BY:

____

____

____

____

____

BUCKET LIST ENTRY #36

Pioneer a Fashion Trend

1. Maybe you wear an interesting bracelet. A pair of jeans ripped just so. An eye patch. A monocle. Perhaps you're a pirate? Do you have any of your own personal fashion choices that are unique to you? What are they?

____

____

____

2. If not, create a new look. Look at your wardrobe. See what others are doing in the world of fashionistaness and try to be unique. Decide what that will be, then continue on this plunge.

____

____

____

3. Have your unique trend? Now come up with a catchy name for your trend and write it down here. Here are a few hypothetically catchy names for fashion trends that don't mean anything but sound fashion-y.

   a. *Ploofy*
   b. *Eye-Jammy*
   c. *Ankleweight 101*
   d. *"The Daryl"*
   e. *Shorts that are also pants*

4. Now you have your name. Good. And by "good" we mean "fabulous." What's next? Start a movement for your trend. Blog/post/tweet/spam your friends and the Internet. And most importantly, make this particular trend your own personal calling card by rocking it all around town. Congratulations on your new signature look!

BUCKET LIST ENTRY #36

I'M GOING TO PLUNGE INTO THE FASHION WORLD, TWO FASHIONABLE FEET FIRST, BY:

BUCKET LIST ENTRY #37

Accomplish the Educational Aspiration of Your Choice

1. Describe your education level.

2. List all of your certifications/letters after your name/awards in your field here (add another page if this space is not sufficient).

3. Marvel at how accomplished you are.

4. Now that you know how accomplished you are, think about how much more accomplished you could still be. Is there something you could do to add to your existing skill set to make you even more proficient? Better yet, is there something completely unrelated you've always wanted to become skilled in? Business? Art? Welding? Whatever it is, commit to something—and put your brain to work immediately.

BUCKET LIST ENTRY #37

I AM GOING TO FIRE MY BRAIN'S SYNAPSES TOWARD SOMETHING NEW THAT'S COOL BY

____

AND ACHIEVING PROFICIENCY AND/OR A CERTIFICATION IN ______________________ .

BUCKET LIST ENTRY #38

Do Something Awesome for Your Family

1. Identify which of these most closely resembles your family:

2. Now that you've identified your family pictorially, describe them with words.

3. True, every family dynamic is different. Some are like relaxing docile gorillas, while others are more akin to badgers badgering each other. Either way, think about something you could do for your family that they would appreciate. Write a family history. Organize a family badminton tournament. Host a family reunion. Design a family coat of arms—complete with oxtail adornments! Whatever it is, make it a contribution the whole family can appreciate.

BUCKET LIST ENTRY #38

I'M GOING TO ACCOMPLISH SOMETHING OF ESPECIALLY MEMORABLE FAMILY VALUE BY:

BUCKET LIST ENTRY #39

Accomplish a Home Project That's Out of Your Normal Comfort Zone

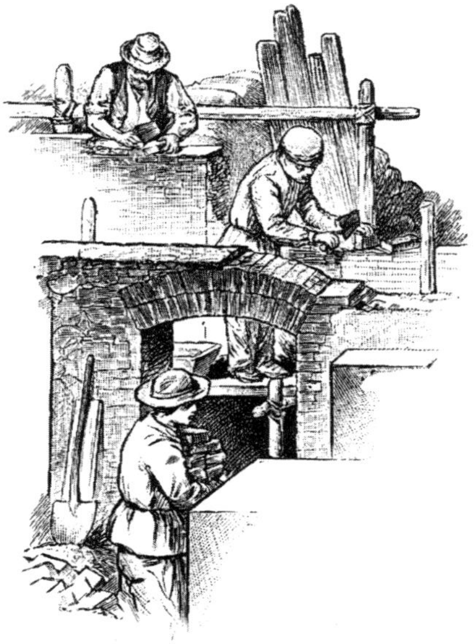

1. List your current dwelling space (home, apartment, condo, teepee).[1]

____

____

____

2. Identify something in or around your home or dwelling that you could improve or upgrade. (If it's a home, maybe you need a new roof or fence built. If it's an apartment, maybe you could use some shelves put up or a room painted. Maybe you just need your bed lofted. Use your imagination.)

____

____

____

[1] If your current dwelling is a hogan, please leave blank.

3. Learn how to do that improvement via classes, helpful in-laws, friends who drink beer while they watch you do the actual work and occasionally give helpful hints through mouthfuls of pizza, etc. Once you've learned, buy the materials. Once you've bought the materials, get your Bob Vila on.

BUCKET LIST ENTRY #39

I'M GOING TO BECOME HANDIER AROUND THE HOUSE THAN I COULD HAVE EVER PREVIOUSLY IMAGINED BY:

BUCKET LIST ENTRY #40

Engage in the Spiritual

1. Take a look at these symbols.

2. How do these symbols make you feel?

3. Have you ever said the word "om" out loud?

- ☐ *Yes*
- ☐ *No*

4. After reflecting on your last two answers, enjoy the realization that you need to explore your spiritual self. After all, life is too fast and furious these days. So here it is: your chance to do something spiritual. If you're religious, make it a religious journey. Visit Israel. Take up yoga. Go to Tibet. Become a monk for a year. Or just take a sabbatical and do nothing for a while. Think of something that will benefit your spiritual self, then do it. You'll be amazed at the inner knowledge and reflection you will gain.

BUCKET LIST ENTRY #40

I'M GOING TO FURTHER MY SPIRITUAL WELL-BEING BY:

____

____

____

____

____

____

____

____

BUCKET LIST ENTRY #41

Attempt to Become Internet Famous

1. Are you already famous on the Internet?

   □ *Yes*
   □ *No*

2. Do you have more than 5,000 Facebook friends?

   □ *Yes*
   □ *No*

3. Are you Mark Zuckerberg?

   □ *Yes*
   □ *No*

4. What would your ideal web achievement be?

   □ *something you wrote*
   □ *a video you made*
   □ *a website you created*
   □ *a blog about birthmarks that look like chairs*

5. Carefully scrutinize your answer above, just as everyone on the Internet is going to scrutinize your work and make you Internet famous.

6. Make that movie. Write that thing. Design that piece. Push it out there. Make it sing. Make it famous. Make it undeniably catchy. Make it viral. And when you get there, don't let it go to your head.[1]

BUCKET LIST ENTRY #41

I'M GOING TO THROW MY HAT INTO THE RING OF INTERNET FAME BY:

____

____

____

____

____

____

____

____

[1] *Helpful tip #1*: Add a cat.

BUCKET LIST ENTRY #42

Attend an Unforgettable Event

1. List a few of your hobbies or interests.

2. Take a look at your list and think about any famous local, nationwide, or even worldwide events that coincide with your interest, for example, the Super Bowl, Sundance, and SXSW.

3. Pick the one event from these that you would most like to attend. The next time it comes up, go. Keep the ticket stub. Make a photo book. Tell everyone you know to look for you on TV.

BUCKET LIST ENTRY #42

ENJOY THE ABILITY, FOR THE REST OF YOUR LIFE, TO SAY, "I WAS THERE" BY:

BUCKET LIST ENTRY #43

Try an Exotic Food

1. Name the most exotic food you have ever eaten.

2. What other exotic foods can you think of that you would never normally consider eating?

3. Identify one you'd be willing to try.

4. Try it and take lots of pictures.

5. Keep it down (this will be the toughest part).

BUCKET LIST ENTRY #43

I'M GOING TO PUT A CURIOUS FOOD IN MY MOUTH THAT I HAD NEVER BEFORE PREVIOUSLY CONSIDERED, SPECIFICALLY IN THE FORM OF:

BUCKET LIST ENTRY #44

Do Something Special for the Holidays

1. During which holidays does your family normally gather for a fun family time?

2. What is your most enjoyed holiday tradition?[1,2]

3. What's your most memorable holiday experience?

[1] It can be any holiday. Including Flag Day.

[2] "Leaving" or "hiding" are acceptable answers.

4. Okay, now it's simple: You're going to top that. For that same holiday you like most, for just one year, make a big deal out of it. If it's Thanksgiving, cook a whole dinner from scratch. If it's Christmas, go skate at Rockefeller Center; if it's Arbor Day, plant an entire forest. Go big or go home.

BUCKET LIST ENTRY #44

I'M GOING TO MAKE A HOLIDAY MOST MEMORABLE BY:

____

____

____

____

____

____

____

____

BUCKET LIST ENTRY #45

Go to the Best Offbeat Gathering You Can Imagine

Lebowski Fest, an annual festival that began in 2002 in Louisville, Kentucky, celebrates Joel and Ethan Coen's 1998 cult film *The Big Lebowski*. During the fest, people wear outfits from the movie, drink White Russians, and go bowling.

1. What is the strangest reason for which you have ever heard of or seen a group of people get together?

____

____

____

____

____

2. Did you actually witness or participate in this? (It's fine if you did. Even if you were wearing a cape. Especially if you were wearing a cape.)

   ☐ *Yes*
   ☐ *No*

3. If not, go see or participate in it the next time you can.

4. If so, pick something else. Anything. What would be even more interesting or weird than what you did attend? Do some research and go. Broaden your horizons. Make new friends. Fly so far past your comfort zone that your comfort zone is waving one hand slowly from side to side asking, longingly, "Friends?" You can nod slowly in return if you like.

BUCKET LIST ENTRY #45

I'M GOING TO BRAVE THE DEPTHS OF A VERY INTERESTING GROUP OF PEOPLE AND ATTEND AND/OR PARTICIPATE IN:

BUCKET LIST ENTRY #46

Go Someplace Foreign and Try to Communicate in a Native Tongue Other Than Your Own

1. List some foreign destinations you've always wanted to visit.

____

____

____

2. Do you speak a foreign language?[1]

☐ *Yes*
☐ *No*

3. Are you willing to learn one, or at least try to pick up enough to get by?

☐ *Yes*
☐ *No*

[1] The "language of love" does not count.

4. If not, go somewhere you've never been and try to get by using only gestures and body language for at least a day or afternoon. Try a completely foreign restaurant in a completely foreign part of town, for instance.[2]

5. If so, choose your language, choose your destination, and make it happen. Keep to a strict rule that you'll stay in their native tongue.

BUCKET LIST ENTRY #46

I'M GOING TO UNLEASH MY INNER FOREIGNER BY:

____

____

____

____

____

[2] Avoid pelvic thrusting, which is a no-no in any language.

BUCKET LIST ENTRY #47

Do the Ultimate Friends Weekend

1. If you were to plan an ultimate "friends weekend," what friends would you want in your entourage?

____

____

____

2. Write down why you would want each friend in said entourage.

____

____

____

3. What do you and your best friend or friends like to do for fun? Wine tasting? Watching basketball tournaments? Running with those guys that run barefoot in South America? Spill it.

____

____

____

4. Take the amp for that fun you normally like to have and turn the fun knob to 11 by planning a weekend with your friends based around said activity.

BUCKET LIST ENTRY #47

I'M GOING TO ORGANIZE THE ULTIMATE FRIENDS WEEKEND BY:

BUCKET LIST ENTRY #48

Experience the Supernatural

1. Check off any of these that you have heard of:

   - ☐ *Loch Ness Monster (Nessie)*
   - ☐ *Bigfoot*
   - ☐ *Sasquatch*
   - ☐ *Yeti*
   - ☐ *Yetisquatch*
   - ☐ *Bear Lake Monster*
   - ☐ *Big Muddy Monster*
   - ☐ *Bloop*
   - ☐ *Chupacabra*
   - ☐ *Devil Bird*
   - ☐ *Flying Rod*
   - ☐ *Giant Ground Sloth*
   - ☐ *Goatman*
   - ☐ *Hoop Snake*
   - ☐ *Jackalope*
   - ☐ *Kraken*
   - ☐ *Mothman*
   - ☐ *Man-Eating Tree*
   - ☐ *Sea Serpent*
   - ☐ *Swamp Ape*
   - ☐ *Will-o'-the-wisp*

2. Do any of these sound like you'd like to meet them? If so, find out where they are rumored to be found and do some "________________________ing" (squatching, nessieing, etc. Make a T-shirt to let everyone know that's what you're doing). Whether you actually find them or not is immaterial.

3. If you'd rather not meet any of these cryptids, go a different route. What interests you about the supernatural? Ghosts? Psychics? Palm readings? Think about it.

4. Seek it out by doing just that. You don't have to go far. After all, the spirits of the supernatural are all around us. As are the Devil Birds.

BUCKET LIST ENTRY #48

I'M GOING TO DO SOMETHING SUPERNATURALLY SUPERAWESOME BY:

____

____

____

____

____

BUCKET LIST ENTRY #49

Eat Something You've Grown Yourself

1. Have you ever grown any foods before? Please describe.

2. If you could grow something yourself, what would it be? Choose something to grow. And if you've already had growing experience, choose something you've never grown before.

3. Grow something yourself—preferably, something you enjoy eating. If you have no garden, use a windowsill. If you have no windowsill, use a community pea patch. If you have no community pea patch, use your imagination.

4. When it's ripe, eat it. But do more than that. Share it. Perfect it. Start growing more of it, if you think others would enjoy it. Become famous. The next thing you know, you'll be running a restaurant called Tao of the Tomato. You're welcome.

BUCKET LIST ENTRY #49

I AM GOING TO GROW ______________________________

SUCCESSFULLY, THEN ENJOY THE FRUITS OF MY WARES (SORRY) BY EATING IT.

BUCKET LIST ENTRY #50

Develop Your Own Catch Phrase

1. Is there something you say all the time? What is it?

   ____

   ____

   ____

2. Did you invent it yourself?

   ☐ *Yes*
   ☐ *No*

3. If so, you've already got your own catch phrase. Just keep pushing it. Make signs. Get it shouted on the local news. Tell it to the most popular men and women at local colleges.

4. If not, invent one. Here are some suffixes to help guide you.

   a. *–town*
   b. *–ocean*
   c. *–ness*
   d. *–someness*
   e. *–hickable!*
   f. *–tastic!*
   g. *–bollyollywolly!*
   h. *–enetrable!*
   i. *–shakalaka!*
   j. *–fricasee!*
   k. *–sauce*
   l. *–beans*
   m. *–corn fritter*
   n. *–vroooooom*

5. Make it stick. Make it famous. Make it something Oprah would want to utter.

BUCKET LIST ENTRY #50

I'M GOING TO DEVELOP MY VERY OWN CATCH PHRASE KNOWN AS ______________________________

____

AND TAKE IT ALL KINDS OF TOTALLY GLOBAL-WIDE.

BUCKET LIST ENTRY #51

Make Your Body Hate You

Not in a bad way. Just via some overindulgence or bad idea that you'll do one single time and never again.

1. Describe the worst thing you've ever put your body through.

2. What's one thing you'd like to do but are afraid of how your body would react? Eat an especially giant burger? Take a polar bear plunge? Run a marathon? Think about the pain and jot it down here.

3. Figure out the safest, least harmful way to accomplish this—then remind yourself it'll be a one-time thing, take a few thousand deep breaths, and do it. Be sure to take the proper precautions, of course, should the need arise.

BUCKET LIST ENTRY #51

I'M GOING TO MAKE AN ENEMY OUT OF MY BODY FOR A VERY SHORT OCCURRENCE OR TIME PERIOD BY:

BUCKET LIST ENTRY #52

Be a Kid Again

1. What's one thing you used to do all the time as a kid that you absolutely loved?

2. Could you do that thing again as an adult while simultaneously avoiding potential embarrassment, scorn, or strange, head-scratching glances? If so, embrace your inner child by rediscovering this activity. Go back to Disneyland. Play with some toys. Build a model of an aircraft carrier.

   If not, do the next closest thing. Buy a new bike. Join an adult sport league for the sport you loved as a kid. And let the innocent childhood memories flow.

BUCKET LIST ENTRY #52

I'm going to be a kid again by:

BUCKET LIST ENTRY #53

Book a Trip Completely Spontaneously

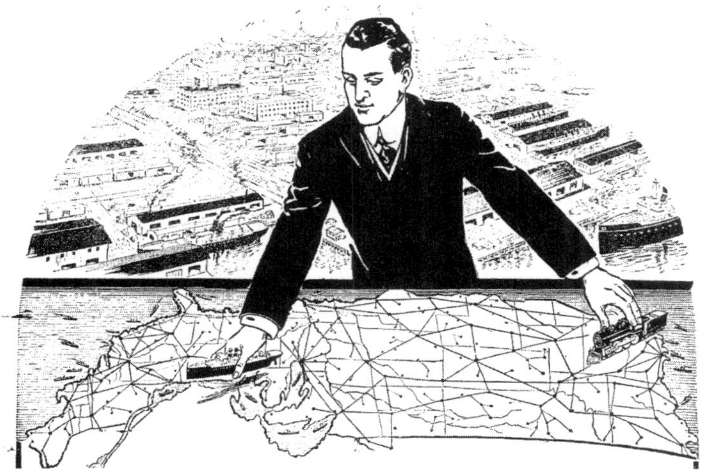

1. Name a destination you have always wanted to go to.

2. Book it. Now. Right now. Seriously. Go.

3. *Stop thinking and start booking!*

BUCKET LIST ENTRY #53

I'M GOING TO THROW CAUTION TO THE TRAVEL WIND BY GOING TO ______________________________

______________________________ ON ____________(date)____________ .

BUCKET LIST ENTRY #54

Throw the Most Original Theme Party Ever

1. What is the coolest theme party you have ever heard about or could possibly conceive?

____

____

____

2. This theme party would/does/has involved: (check all that apply)[1]

- ☐ *wearing a hat that makes the wearer look like a fish*
- ☐ *gold chains and/or gold doubloons (ideally, both)*
- ☐ *ice cream, socially (not to be confused with an Ice Cream Social, which is different)*
- ☐ *Tusken Raiders*
- ☐ *doing the Hand Jive, that crazy Hand Jive*

[1] If none of the above apply/applied, that's fine—it's *your* book and *your* party. (Cry if you want to.)

3. Have you ever been to one of the party types listed in Question 1? If not, host one—either at your abode or the abode of your friends, relatives, coworkers, or drunken uncle. If so, think of something even cooler than what you just thought of.

BUCKET LIST ENTRY #54

I'M GOING TO HOST THE COOLEST, MOST CREATIVE, MOST ORIGINAL SHINDIG, SOIREE, OR JAMBOREE BY:

BUCKET LIST ENTRY #55

Become One with Nature

1. When you hear "outdoors," do you think "the great outdoors"?

   ☐ *Yes*
   ☐ *No*

2. When you hear "the great outdoors," do you think of John Candy and, to a lesser extent, Stephanie Faracy?

   ☐ *Yes*
   ☐ *No*

3. Think about everything our great nature-filled world has to offer (besides vicious bears and the flopping, slippery salmon that are occasionally held in the grasp of bears). If you could go outdoors and do something you've never done before, what would it be?

   ____

   ____

   ____

Get off your duff and go do it. Maybe it's bungee jumping. Maybe it's going on an epic hike. Maybe it's seeing every single species of bird in the entire tri-state metro Des Moines area on a random sunny Saturday. Whatever it is, make it happen—and make it memorable.

4. If it's impossible to go do it, due to lack of funds, travel logistics, or the fact that you made something up that doesn't exist (balancing on tendrils, for example), find the coolest thing you can do locally—free. You'll surprise yourself with your creativity while simultaneously realizing that nature, unlike those headphones Dr. Dre makes, can be amazingly affordable.

BUCKET LIST ENTRY #55

I'M GOING TO TURN THE GREAT OUTDOORS INTO THE GREATEST OUTDOORS EXPERIENCE I'VE EVER HAD IN MY LIFE BY:

____

____

____

____

____

____

____

BUCKET LIST ENTRY #56

Teach a Class on Your Unique Knowledge about Something

1. What subject do you have a particularly extensive and/or unique knowledge about? Examples: hip-hop music history and lyric analysis, geometry, refuting Columbus.

2. Is this subject "fishing"? If so, pick something else. There are too many fishing teachers out there as it is.

3. What is it about your subject that you'd like to teach others? Why are *you* so interested in it? What would you like people to learn about it?

4. Share your knowledge. Is it something you can teach as a class? Lecture? Mini-lecture? Mini-lecture at a lectern? Write a book. Write an article. Anything you can do to get what's in your brain out and into the waiting, outstretched brains of others.

BUCKET LIST ENTRY #56

I'M GOING TO ENGAGE IN UNIQUE KNOWLEDGE BRAIN-TRANSFER BY:

BUCKET LIST ENTRY #57

Cut Back on Technology Usage for a While

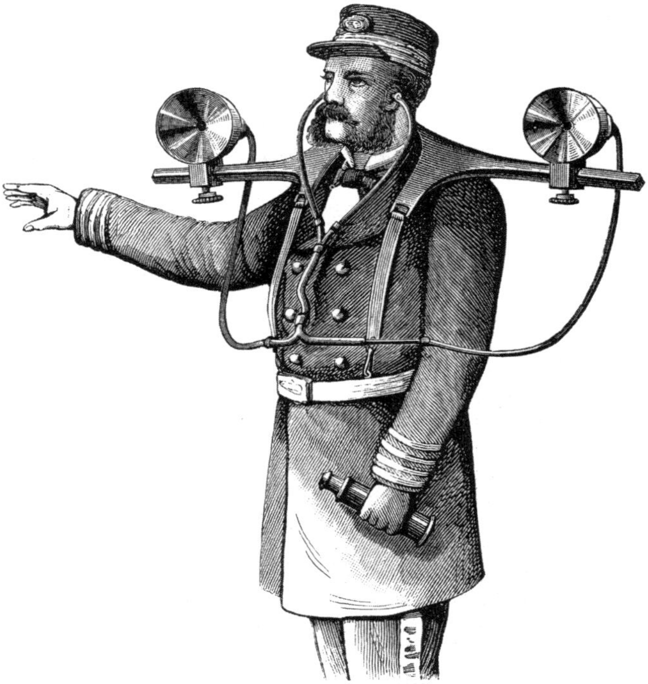

1. Have you ever wished e-mail would grow arms and slap you in the face for using it so much?

2. Choose a form of technology of which you are currently a heavy user and decide on a concerted, definitive way to cut it off or cut it back. "No work e-mail on Fridays after 6," "No cell phone calls while I'm on the train," or "I will stop watching reruns of *The Adventures of Briscoe County, Jr.* until my hands shake" are all great ways to get started. Write your answer down here.

____

____

____

3. Use this universal symbol for "no" and write what technology you're leaving behind behind that symbol. See examples to help guide you.

Examples:

No e-mail while I'm watching a movie
No cloud computing while bicycle riding
No reruns of The Adventures of Briscoe County, Jr.

BUCKET LIST ENTRY #57

I'M GOING TO LESSEN MY VIRTUAL REALITY SO I CAN STRENGTHEN MY REAL REALITY BY:

BUCKET LIST ENTRY #58

Organize a Rally or an Event for Something That Matters to You

1. Describe a time when you felt extremely passionate about something.

2. Name a humanitarian passion you feel strongly about.

3. Describe why you feel so strongly about that passion.

4. Have you ever organized a rally or event for this passion or cause in the past? If not, do it. If so, do it again, but this time do it bigger and grander. Up the stakes. Get the word out even more. *The world needs to know.*

BUCKET LIST ENTRY #58

I'M GOING TO MAKE A DIFFERENCE FOR THE CAUSE OF

BY

BUCKET LIST ENTRY #59

Experience the Ultimate Loss of Inhibition

1. Describe a time when you felt you truly lost your inhibitions.

2. What were the short- and long-term effects of doing so?

3. List something you would never, ever, in the world do. In fact, list three things.

4. Take a look at your list. Are any of these things illegal? If so, cross out the illegal ones. Are all of these things illegal? If so, cross out all of them and list three more things. Continue this process in perpetuity *ad infinitum* until you are left with a non-crossed-out answer.

5. Whatever is crossed out or listed last on your list, that's the one you're doing, Sluggo. So do it.

BUCKET LIST ENTRY #59

I'M GOING TO SURPRISE THE BEJEEZUS OUT OF MYSELF, AND EVERYONE WHO KNOWS ME, BY PLAYING OPPOSITE DAY WITH MY SELF-CONSCIOUSNESS AND:

BUCKET LIST ENTRY #60

Perform an Amazing Favor for a Stranger

1. Think about a time a stranger surprised you by doing some sort of favor. Describe what it was and what it felt like.

____

____

____

____

____

2. Which of these best describes the pedestal on which you would put this stranger after doing whatever favor he or she did for you:[1]

☐ *a pedestal next to Michael Jordan*
☐ *a pedestal next to Johnny Cash*
☐ *a pedestal next to Hank Azaria*

[1] Every answer is right.

3. What's something you could do for a stranger, or better yet, a group of strangers, that would be unexpected and would also cause them to consider putting you on a Jordanesque pedestal as well? Could you feed some parking meters for strangers for the heck of it? Buy coffee for the next five people in line? Fill someone's car with gas? Go ahead, get your love for a random human on.

BUCKET LIST ENTRY #60

I'M GOING TO PAY IT FORWARD (WITH OR WITHOUT THE PARTICIPATION OF SUSAN SARANDON OR HALEY JOEL OSMENT) BY:

BUCKET LIST ENTRY #61

Attempt to Crash or Sneak Into an Event[1]

1. Pick your preferred disguise:

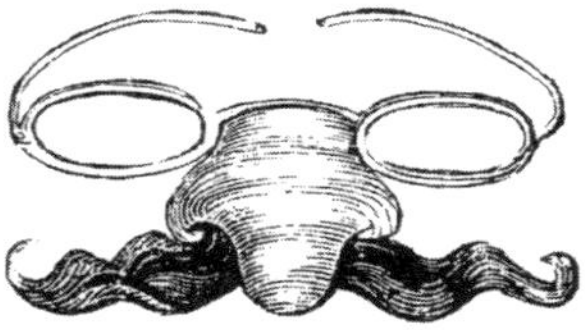

2. What event do you think you would have the most fun crashing? Wedding? Company party? Sporting event? Backstage at a show?

___

___

___

[1] Please note that by reading this page you agree that the author and illustrator of *Make Your Own Bucket List*, publisher of same, editor of same, agent of same, mother of same, father of same, brother with a strange addiction to pretzels of same, dog that resembles Ted Turner of same, ungrateful grandkids of same, and President Obama's dog Bo can in no way be held liable for any event crashing that results in bodily harm, injury, arrest, or prosecution.

3. Think of an out. What's your excuse if you get caught? What do you say? Can you guarantee you won't get prosecuted?

4. Try it. Either by yourself or with a friend. Whichever yields the best odds and chance for fun. And if you get caught, don't say we didn't warn you.

BUCKET LIST ENTRY #61

I'M GOING TO BE SOMEONE I'M NOT BY CRASHING:

BUCKET LIST ENTRY #62

Surprise a Sweetie Romantically

1. Do you have a sweetie?

   ☐ *Yes*
   ☐ *No*

2. Rephrasing the question: Do you have a pooky, pokey, snookums, babe, sweetums, snookerwerts, smooshy-wooshy, honey, honey bee, or little honey ham hock?

   ☐ *Yes*
   ☐ *No*

3. What's the most surprising thing you've ever done for a significant other?

   ____

   ____

   ____

4. After all this questioning, do you still have a significant other?

   ☐ *Yes*
   ☐ *No*

5. If so, plan something you've never done before from a romantic standpoint and surprise your other with it. Plan a dinner on the beach. Cater an entire meal in the back of a U-Haul truck. Set up six TVs in your living room, all of which play *The Notebook* (but start them all at different points in the movie). If not, *treat yourself* to something in the same vein but completely spontaneously.

BUCKET LIST ENTRY #62

I'M GOING TO SPRING AN UNEXPECTED ACT FROM THE PLANET LOVETRON UPON MY UNSUSPECTING PARTNER OR, ABSENT A PARTNER, MYSELF BY:

BUCKET LIST ENTRY #63

Emcee an Event

1. Are you an auctioneer?

   - ☐ *Yes*
   - ☐ *No*

2. Are you a hog caller?

   - ☐ *Yes*
   - ☐ *No*

3. Are you both? If you are both, please go lie down and keep your greatness away from the rest of us.

4. If you are one of the two, then do nothing; this entry on your bucket list has already been checked in triplicate.

5. Based on your life right now, what are some opportunities you can think of for stepping up, grabbing the mic, and entertaining the crowd?

6. If you are not an auctioneer or a professional hog caller, fret not. Think about opportunities in which you could control a microphone and entertain. Everyone should have this experience once. It gives you the opportunity to wax nostalgic. Engage in platitudes. Pontificate. You will have the audience's attention! How will you command it? At an upcoming friend's wedding? A bat mitzvah? A bar mitzvah? A company party? Your dad's retirement party? Decide!

BUCKET LIST ENTRY #63

I'M GOING TO WIELD THE MICROPHONE LIKE A SCEPTER AND HOLD COURT BY EMCEEING:

____

____.[1]

[1] Also, I will not tell bad jokes like that "Not your cheese/Nacho cheese" one that everyone seems to be telling these days.

BUCKET LIST ENTRY #64

Plan the Ultimate Dinner

1. How would you define the ultimate dinner?

____

____

____

2. Who would be doing the cooking?

____

____

____

3. Would pants be a requirement for said ultimate dinner?

☐ *Yes*
☐ *No*

4. Who would you want to be there? Gandhi?

____

____

____

5. Would your idea of an ultimate dinner be Sbarro?

   - ☐ *Yes*
   - ☐ *No*

6. Plan the ultimate dinner. At home, at a restaurant, at your favorite friend's house, which has a game room the size of Safeco Field. It's your rules. Your guidelines. Your way. Invite who you want. Serve what you want. Be all you can be.

BUCKET LIST ENTRY #64

I'M GOING TO PLAN A DINNER EXPERIENCE ON THE GRANDEST OF GRAND SCALES BY:

BUCKET LIST ENTRY #65

Become Proficient in a New Computer Skill

1. List your current computer skills.
   Examples: MS Word, MS Access, MS Labrador Retriever finder, Googling "Bigfoot."

   ____

   ____

   ____

2. What is missing from this list that you wish were there?

   ____

   ____

   ____

3. Take your best guess at what this is saying to you IN CODE.

   00001111100000000000000000111110000000000000000000000000000000000000000000000000000000000
   000000000000000000000000000000001

4. Coding?

5. Pick a computer skill you want to learn and learn it—from an expert, from a class, from the Internet itself. It could be something you answered for answer Number 2, or it could be something else. Whatever you choose, learn it—and make those little boxes of technological glad-handing do something more for you.

BUCKET LIST ENTRY #65

I'M GOING TO DEVELOP A NEWFANGLED COMPUTER SKILL BY:

____

____

____

____

____

____

____

BUCKET LIST ENTRY #66

Spend a Day Doing a Job That Is the Polar Opposite of Your Job

1. What is your job?[1]

2. What tasks are required of you to excel at your job?

[1] "Student" okay, "Unemployed" okay, "General Sainthood" not okay (with exceptions, Saint Peter).

3. Gaze back at your previous answer. Think about the skills you use. Then, think about skills you possess but *never* use at work: Math. Physical activity. Line dancing. Next, identify a job title or description that makes use of one or some of these. For our intents and purposes, we will consider this job *the opposite* of your job.

4. Figure out how to do what you listed above as a job for a day—whether it's paid or unpaid, real or simulated, or involving actual manure cleanup versus imagined manure cleanup. Congratulations! Career enlightenment is officially yours.

BUCKET LIST ENTRY #66

I'M GOING TO TAKE AN EMPLOYMENT DETOUR BY PERFORMING, FOR ONE DAY, A TOTALLY NEW JOB DESCRIPTION KNOWN AS:

BUCKET LIST ENTRY #67

Accomplish Something Photographically

1. Determine the favorite photograph you have ever taken.

____

____

____

2. Can you determine a favorite photograph?

☐ *Yes*
☐ *No*

3. If yes, tell us about it here. If no, find a favorite photograph someone else has shot. Now call that your favorite photograph. Hug it, care for it, nurture it, frame it, display it, show it to your mother-in-law, show it to your friends on the street, hang it above your bed, and try to sneak it into a museum. But first, describe your favorite photograph here.

____

____

____

____

____

4. Share your favorite photograph with the world. Can you get it into a museum? A gallery? An amateur show? The Louvre? The International Cryptozoology Museum in Portland, Maine? A college dorm room? An airplane? An airplane bathroom? Your boss's office? Find a way you can share it with the outside world on as grand a scale as you can.

BUCKET LIST ENTRY #67

I'm going to show off a photographic magnum opus by:

BUCKET LIST ENTRY #68

Experience the Epic Outdoors

1. What is your favorite thing about being outdoors?

____

____

____

2. When you're doing what you love outdoors, which of the following expressions are you most likely to encounter: (check all that apply)

- ☐ *"That's some fresh pow pow!"*
- ☐ *"Shaka, brah!"*
- ☐ *"Skate or die!"*
- ☐ *"Excuse me, my son is riding a unicycle and needs to get by"*
- ☐ *"Contrary to my beard and hood, I am not the Unabomber"*
- ☐ *"Where's my mountain lion?"*
- ☐ *"I didn't know they made Clif Bars from the hairy leg follicles of professional Sherpas! Tangy!"*
- ☐ *"Monkeys!"*

3. What is your overall favorite thing to do or see outdoors?

____

____

____

4. Think about a way you can push your answer from the previous question to the limits. If your favorite outdoor activity is rafting, go on an epic rafting trip. If it's surfing, go surf the North Shore; if it's visiting national parks, go on a mini-tour to the very coolest ones you've never seen.

BUCKET LIST ENTRY #68

I'M GOING TO TAKE MY FAVORITE OUTDOOR ACTIVITY TO A WHOLE NEW LEVEL BY:

BUCKET LIST ENTRY #69

Make Your Own Ad

1. What's your favorite commercial in the history of commercials?[1]

2. What product or service would you most like to make a commercial or do an advertisement for?

3. Why do you love it so much? Is it the idea? The tagline? What?

[1] Please mention what this favorite commercial is advertising, rather than just saying, "It's that one with the ninjas serving pop-top espresso drinks from the top of the Empire State Building while breakdancing." Though we agree, that one does sound pretty awesome.

4. Why did you choose this product or service? What is it about it that you think is worthy of being advertised?

5. Do it. Think up the idea, write a commercial script, film it, and put it online. Or design a poster and put it up. Boom, you're just like all the characters in *Mad Men*, minus the black sporting jackets, business hats, and copious philandering.

BUCKET LIST ENTRY #69

I'M GOING TO CREATE A CREATIVE, FUN, AND POSSIBLY MEMORABLE COMMERCIAL PIECE FOR PUBLIC CONSUMPTION BY:

BUCKET LIST ENTRY #70

Try an Extreme Sport

1. Have you ever engaged in an extreme sport?[1]

   ☐ *Yes*
   ☐ *No*

2. Have you ever invented an extreme sport?[2]

   ☐ *Yes*
   ☐ *No*

3. Scan your brain, mind, and the Internet for all the extreme sports you can think of. Decide which one sounds the most fun, feasible, and/or least awful and try it.

BUCKET LIST ENTRY #70

I'M GOING TO BECOME *EXTREEEEEEME* IN THE WORLD OF EXTREME SPORTS BY:

____

____

____

____

____

[1] By extreme sport, we mean something that's not one of your traditional sports but something more interesting and/or crazier than those. It's a broad definition, so think slowly.

[2] Again, you may surprise yourself. Because the Milk Chug Challenge *totally* counts.

BUCKET LIST ENTRY #71

Entertain Children on a Grand Scale

1. Children find you:

   - ☐ *fun*
   - ☐ *silly*
   - ☐ *confusing*
   - ☐ *overly bearded*

2. Kids are full of innocence and wonder. More importantly, they tend to be easily entertained by grownups—especially grownups who don't mind making fools of themselves. Pick something fun you could do for a group (say ten or so) of kids: dress up as a clown for a birthday party, be a magician, sing a song, put on a play, take them all to a baseball game, coach a Little League team, and so on. Cast the net wide, and remember—it's for the kids!

BUCKET LIST ENTRY #71

I'm going to give some kids the opportunity to experience ten tons of fun on my watch by:

____

____

____

____

____

BUCKET LIST ENTRY #72

Attend the Ultimate Sporting Event

1. What is your favorite sport?[1]

2. If you don't have a favorite sport, which one will you at least tolerate without making your eyes spit back at you inwardly with frustration?

3. What is the ultimate pinnacle of greatness in your favorite sport? Is it the Super Bowl? The Olympics? The world international championships of some sort?

[1] Couch surfing and "throwing ragers" are not considered sports. Tigermilking is.

4. Procure a ticket and attend it. And if you can't, go to the next closest ultimate pinnacle, maybe a playoff game or a more local championship. Regardless of the sport or venue, it's going to be an unforgettable and interesting people-watching experience.

BUCKET LIST ENTRY #72

I'M GOING TO WITNESS SPORTS HISTORY BY:

BUCKET LIST ENTRY #73

Invest in Something

1. Pick something you would want to invest in.

2. Take a look at your finances. A long, hard look. Figure out how much of your take-home salary you could set aside, per month, for an investment. Any amount is okay, even $0. But try your best to make it some nonzero amount.

3. How much money do you spend per month on ice cream sandwiches?

____

____

4. New basketballs?

____

____

5. Good.

6. Make a commitment to set aside the amount you have decided on for one full year. After that year, evaluate how your investment is doing. Adjust, continue, or start over as results dictate. Be patient. And if you can't set aside anything of value now, keep investing in the back of your mind and return to this entry as soon as you can.

BUCKET LIST ENTRY #73

I'M GOING TO TAKE THE LONG VIEW WITH MY MONEY BY INVESTING ______*(amount per month)*______

IN ______________________*(investment type)*______________________

____

____

____ .

BUCKET LIST ENTRY #74

Take an Amtrak Train Somewhere

1. Look at the Amtrak route map. From where you live, where could you go?

    ____

    ____

    ____

2. Of the places you listed, do you have the desire to go to any of these places?

    ☐ *Yes*
    ☐ *No*

3. Do you have a periodic urge to yell "Choo-choo!" loudly while standing next to the conductor and/or actually driving the train itself?

    ☐ *Yes*
    ☐ *No*

4. If you answered no—*liar!*

5. If you have the desire to go any of the places you can go, and it's a reasonably long trip (read: >5 hours), do it! If not, reconsider, then do it. Because *everyone* should take a long train trip at least once in their lives. When we're talking trains, it's less about the destination and more about the journey.

And while you are on board, live it up. Befriend the porter. Try the mysterious thing called "train food." Meet and shake hands with real hoboes. You're a rail rider now!

BUCKET LIST ENTRY #74

RIDE THE AMTRAK CORPORATION IRON HORSE SOMEWHERE INTERESTING BY:

____

____

____

____

____

BUCKET LIST ENTRY #75

Organize a Pamper Day

1. What's the most overindulgent way to pamper yourself that you could possibly think of? Nothing is too overindulgent.

____

____

____

2. To prove nothing is too overindulgent, consider the plottings below and note how they lay out on this indulgence graph.

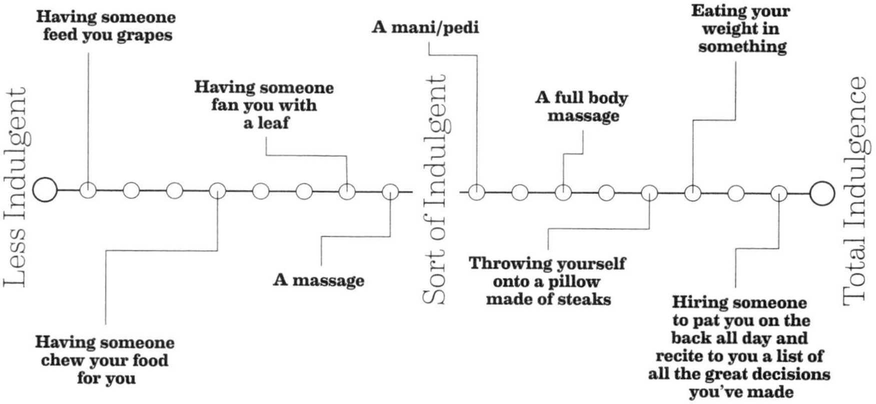

3. Get it now? Good. Go pamper.

BUCKET LIST ENTRY #75

I'M GOING TO OVERINDULGE OR PAMPER MYSELF THE BEST WAY I KNOW HOW, WHICH WOULD BE:

BUCKET LIST ENTRY #76

Find Your Signature Cocktail

1. What is your favorite liquor? If you don't drink alcohol, what is your favorite drink? You can always invent something of the virgin variety.

___

___

___

2. What are your favorite general flavors? List all you can think of—sweet, sour, bitter, whatever.

___

___

___

3. What are your favorite drink accessories? Olives, bitters, lemon slice, mini umbrellas, etc.

___

___

___

4. Do some research or your own experimentation based on the above and decide on . . . your *signature cocktail*. You can invent one, or just commit to an existing one that you love a lot. Either way is fine, just commit. This is a big moment. Your goal here is to become known for your drink, one way or another. You'll be like James Bond!

BUCKET LIST ENTRY #76

My signature cocktail is:____________________________________

It contains: ____________________________________

BUCKET LIST ENTRY #77

Create Your Own Special Recipe for a Food You Love

1. What is your favorite food?

2. What is the best version of that food you ever had? Where? Why?

3. Make this food for yourself. Only this time, add a little something different to it. Buy some things, do some tastings, experiment. Show it to someone else; have him or her try it. Serve it at a dinner for your family. Soon your trial-and-error recipe will become the next big thing and you'll be turning away offers to partner with Target's food court conglomerate.

4. How adept are you at preparing this food for yourself? Describe some ways you've made it. How has it gone?

5. Is someone you know better at making this food than you? How does he or she do it? Could you borrow his or her recipe, then put your own twist on it?

BUCKET LIST ENTRY #77

I'm going to make a food I love into a unique culinary mouth party by:

BUCKET LIST ENTRY #78

Commit to a New Diet for a Month

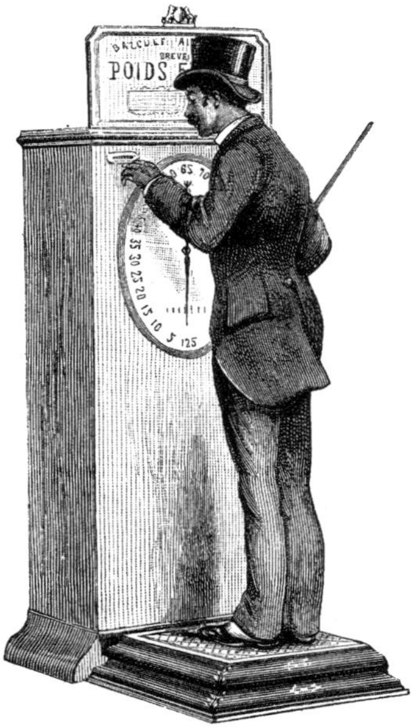

1. Describe any diets you've been on in the past. How did they work?

2. Have you ever been over to Jared the Subway guy's house for dinner?

   ☐ *Yes*
   ☐ *No*

3. If so, did he have a train room?

4. Is there a diet out there that you are especially curious about? Or just one that someone you know has followed and had some success with?

5. Find out more about that diet. Commit to it for a month. Lock down your cravings. Engage in person-to-refrigerator combat. Adjust to a temporary nonmeat existence. And in the end, see what happens. And it's important to note that this doesn't in any way need to be about losing weight. With food, as with everything else, it's easy to fall into expected, tried-and-true habits and meals. Here's your chance to step outside that comfort zone.

BUCKET LIST ENTRY #78

I'M GOING TO SUCCEED IN OVERHAULING MY DIETARY WANTS AND NEEDS BY:

BUCKET LIST ENTRY #79

Maintain or Cultivate a Family Tradition to Pass Down

1. Do you want to be remembered by your family for generations to come?

   ☐ *Yes*
   ☐ *No*

2. Do you want to be more memorable than the famous Wheaties cereal-advertising slogan, "The Breakfast of Champions"?

   ☐ *Yes*
   ☐ *No*

3. Do you even think that's humanly possible?

   ☐ *Yes*
   ☐ *No*

4. Okay, then.

5. Write down some family traditions you've participated in over the years.

   ____

   ____

   ____

6. Which one is your favorite?

7. Is this a tradition that you could proudly pass down with gusto to your next generation of family members? If so, let the tires of family legacy rotate on. If not, invent your own *new* tradition. This could potentially be the more fun and creative route, because it's an open book. Proclaim a new favorite family restaurant. Start a yearly trip tradition to the local trout museum. Make up your own holiday. Isn't family awesome?

BUCKET LIST ENTRY #79

I AM GOING TO CEMENT MY FAMILY LEGACY FOR GENERATIONS TO COME BY:

BUCKET LIST ENTRY #80

Become a Local Expert

1. You consider where you live to be:

    a. *a point of pride*
    b. *a point of contention*
    c. *Albuquerque*

2. Assuming you take at least a smidgen, a dollop, or a scintilla of pride in where you live, geographically speaking, what are some of the things your city, neighborhood, or general area is known for?

____

____

____

____

____

3. Which of the above local interests do you share?

4. If you answered with one local interest, pursue that and become an expert. If there's more than one, pick the one that sounds the most interesting. If your answer is "none," "zero," or "covering large awnings with paint chips," that's fine, for you must grow your knowledge base anyway! Taking an interest in one of these local delights that you wouldn't normally care about can only serve to broaden the gourds of your general life interest cornucopia. In other words, pick one anyway and learn about it.

BUCKET LIST ENTRY #80

I'M GOING TO BECOME A LOCAL IN THE KNOW, TO THE POINT THAT WHEN AN OUTSIDER COMES TO TOWN I'M ARMED TO THE TEETH WITH KNOWLEDGE MISSILES, BY:

BUCKET LIST ENTRY #81

Go on the Ultimate Romantic Getaway

1. When it comes to love, do you consider yourself to be a romantic by nature?

   ☐ *Yes*
   ☐ *No*

2. What's the most romantic thing you've ever done?

   ____

   ____

   ____

3. Describe your ideal romantic getaway.[1]

   ____

   ____

   ____

[1] This is important: you needn't be romantically attached to answer this, or even to do it, for that matter. You can still find some romance in being with yourself. (Hmm, that may have came out wrong. But we think you see what we're getting at here.)

4. If you have a partner, would she/he agree with your assessment? Because if not, your ideal romantic time may not wind up being quite so much.

   ☐ *Yes*
   ☐ *No*

5. Plan it. Do it. Love it. But first, have some conversations. If it's with a partner, compromise so there's something for both of you to enjoy. If it's by yourself, consider it a *treat-yourself* kind of weekend and get your self-spoiling on (again, not necessarily in *that* way).

BUCKET LIST ENTRY #81

I'M GOING TO ENJOY THE ULTIMATE ROMANTIC GETAWAY BY:

____

____

____

____

____

____

____

BUCKET LIST ENTRY #82

Become the Ultimate Movie Buff

1. No one can see every movie. But you *can* become a certain *type* of movie expert, depending on your interests. Do you have a favorite movie subject (gorillas, hip-hop, gorilla hip-hop, movies about snack cakes)?

2. Do you have a favorite movie director?

3. Which one interests you more: becoming a movie buff about a certain subject, or becoming a movie buff about your favorite director?

____

____

____

4. There's your answer! It's right on this page!!

BUCKET LIST ENTRY #82

I'M GOING TO BECOME A WALKING MOTION PICTURE AUTHORITY FIGURE IN THE ARENA OF

____ .

BY WATCHING THESE FILMS (LIST FILMS HERE, MINIMUM TEN MOVIES):

______________________ ______________________

______________________ ______________________

______________________ ______________________

______________________ ______________________

______________________ ______________________

______________________ ______________________

______________________ ______________________

______________________ ______________________

______________________ ______________________

______________________ ______________________

BUCKET LIST ENTRY #83

Do Something Meaningful for Your Country

1. Circle which picture most closely resembles your level of patriotism.

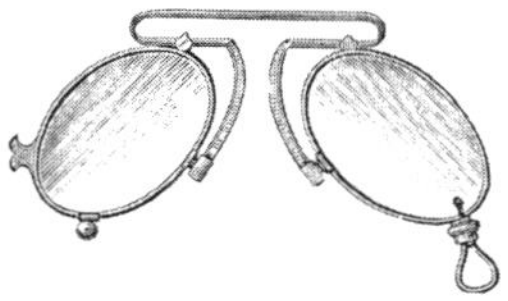

2. List some things you've done in the past for your country. Did you serve in the military? Did you volunteer at the ballot box for an election? Did you volunteer at a soup kitchen? It could be any wide range of answers, and it should be. After all, helping your country can mean a lot of different things.

3. Look at your list. Is it barren? Is it empty? Is it chock full of country pride? If it's barren or empty, scrutinize the events currently going on in the world. What could you do to help your country? Think about it, write down your answer here, and commit to it. And if your list is already chock full, think about something you haven't done yet. Either way, you're being a dutiful citizen, and your country would be proud of you. And so would JFK for bringing his famous quote to life.

BUCKET LIST ENTRY #83

I'M GOING TO WEAR MY COUNTRY PRIDE ON MY PATRIOTIC SLEEVE BY:

BUCKET LIST ENTRY #84

Take an Epic Trip with a Relative

1. Name the person related to you that you enjoy spending time with the most.[1]

2. What is it about this relative that makes you enjoy his or her company so much? Please be more specific than "because she bakes the finest scones in many counties."

3. What kinds of things do you and your favorite relative like to do together?

[1] Spouse not okay; in-laws totally okay, and actually, more than totally okay—we're really impressed with you, in fact. Boy.

4. Choose a potential trip or vacation destination based on any of your shared interests. (You both like wine, you both like sports, you both like seeing Kenny G in concert, etc.) Go for it! You'll become even closer (like family should!) than you already were. If not, talk to this relation and arrive at a fun answer. Then, go do your thang. Huzzah for family!

BUCKET LIST ENTRY #84

I'm going to go on a memorable trip with a favorite familial relation by:

BUCKET LIST ENTRY #85

Make a Household Item or Piece of Furniture from Scratch

1. Your skills with tools or projects around the house would best be described as:

   - ☐ *"Bob Vila on steroids."*
   - ☐ *"Viking-like."*
   - ☐ *"Single-celled amoeba."*
   - ☐ *"Fermented shark."*

2. What household skills *are* you good at? List any that apply. Including folding laundry and trash maintenance.

   ____

   ____

   ____

3. When was the last time you tried to make something? Did you once take a pottery class? Ever done a little woodworking in the garage? Did you slice open your fingertip on the band saw in eighth grade shop class?

   ____

   ____

   ____

4. Pick an item around the house that you would be willing to attempt to make. It could be anything from a knickknack such as a small picture frame or birdhouse to a chair or even dining room table.

   What supplies, knowledge, and supervision would you need to make this item? Do some research and list them all here. Once you've collected what you need to collect (including a class or two, if applicable), make it happen.

___

___

___

BUCKET LIST ENTRY #85

I'M GOING TO CREATE, WITH MY OWN TWO HANDS, SOMETHING FOR MY HOME. THAT SOMETHING WILL BE:

___

___

___

___

___

BUCKET LIST ENTRY #86

Experience the Most Personal Music Experience of Your Life

1. What's the most intimate way you've ever connected with music?

____

____

____

2. Describe some possibilities.

____

____

____

3. Would you end the performance with jazz hands, or jazz feet?

☐ *Yes*
☐ *No*

If so, circle the one you would end the performance with.

4. Music. Makes the people. Come together. This much is true. But would it be possible to take your music love to an entirely new, entirely more intimate, entirely more personal level? We say yes. Think about a way to connect with musicians like you never have before. Spitball a little bit and write down some possibilities here.

   Could you get backstage? Could you meet the musician or musicians? Could you have the musician or musicians over to your house to perform? Could you *play* with the musician or musicians for other people?

   ____

   ____

   ____

5. Look at your list. See what's possible. Decide what would be the most memorable to you. Do it and enjoy a music-themed night that's as memorable as it is melodic.

BUCKET LIST ENTRY #86

I'M GOING TO MAKE AN EXTRAORDINARY MUSIC MEMORY BY:

____

____

____

____

____

BUCKET LIST ENTRY #87

Write the Best, Most Meaningful, Most Compelling Letter You've Ever Written

1. Would you consider yourself to be a good writer?

   ☐ *Yes*
   ☐ *No*

2. When was the last time you wrote a letter to someone? To whom was it addressed?

   ____

   ____

   ____

3. If you could write a letter to anyone, who would it be?

   ____

   ____

   ____

4. Write an open letter to that person. Keep it concise, but pour your heart out. Check your grammar, but paint a picture in your own words. Think about this letter as your Grand Teton of the written word—as if it will be read by millions of people. Because if it's good enough, maybe it will be.

5. Send your letter. Snail-mail first, of course, as that's still the gold-letter-sending standard. But after that, post it online, too. Circulate it among friends. See if it gains any traction. Perhaps, lo and behold, you've just written something that takes off organically and gains you followers, well-wishers, and glad handers by the quazillions, and before you know it you shuffle off to Nantucket to write about why baseball is no longer the grand old game. It could happen!

BUCKET LIST ENTRY #87

I'M GOING TO WRITE MY MOST COMPELLING PIECE OF PROSE YET, AND IT'S GOING TO BE ABOUT:

____

____

____

____

____

IT'S GOING TO BE ADDRESSED TO: ______________________________

BUCKET LIST ENTRY #88

Engage in Some Sort of Secret Spy Activity

1. Are you a member of the KGB or a ninja?

   ☐ *Yes*
   ☐ *No*

2. Assuming not, everyone should do some kind of amateur spying in their lifetime. Name someone you would want to spy on.

   ____

   ____

   ____

3. Traverse the Internet or locate your nearest local spy store to get some supplies and ideas. What equipment looks interesting or useful to you?

4. Pick a target and tail them for a few hours. Get some binoculars and watch some neighbors for a bit and see if anything interesting happens. "Wire yourself up" for an important conversation and see if you can get away with it.[1] Then, write down everything that happens in the space below. Don't get discovered! This message will self-destruct in ten seconds.

BUCKET LIST ENTRY #88

I WILL ENGAGE IN A *SUPERSECRET* COVERT SPY OPERATION BY:

[1] Check the eavesdropping laws in your state first. Some states (we call them "spoilsports") don't look too kindly on unauthorized, supersecret covert operations.

BUCKET LIST ENTRY #89

Relive a Specific Historic Event

1. What is your favorite historical time period?

2. Who is your favorite historical figure?

3. Name some famous historical events that are of particular interest to you.

4. Could you reenact, relive, or revisit any of these historical events where they happened? Is there a historic site there? Is there a museum? Is there a rec center?

5. Examine your answers to the above. Travel to the physical location that makes the most sense, or that you have the highest degree of passion for, and relive the event.

BUCKET LIST ENTRY #89

I'M GOING TO CHECK OUT SOMETHING AMAZING IN HISTORY, WHILE EXAMINING JUST THE WAY IT HAPPENED, BY:

BUCKET LIST ENTRY #90

Get on TV

1. Is there anything you could do that would somehow convince a local news channel to have you on as a guest?

2. Could you figure out a way to sneak into a news report?

3. Could you figure out a way to become a TV weatherman? Please, tell us!

4. Could you perform some sort of spectacle, or wear some sort of outfit so memorable, or otherwise become so polarizing, irritating, or otherwise news-making that a TV station somewhere would be given no choice but to shove a camera in your face?

   - ☐ *Yes*
   - ☐ *No*

5. If you can answer yes to any of the above, make it happen. If not, you just aren't trying hard enough. Start juggling or riding a unicycle, and for Solomon's sake, be persistent! *The news will come calling.*

BUCKET LIST ENTRY #90

I'm going to finagle my way onto television by:

____

____

____

____

____

BUCKET LIST ENTRY #91

Travel in Style

1. What do you like most about traveling?

2. What do you like the least?

3. What would be your preferred mode of transportation when traveling:

- ☐ *first-class flight*
- ☐ *Amtrak sleeper car*
- ☐ *Smart car*
- ☐ *Smart cart*
- ☐ *limousine*
- ☐ *Land Rover*
- ☐ *horse and buggy*
- ☐ *donkey*

4. For once in you're life, you're going to travel in the style you want. Whichever answer you picked above, the next time you travel somewhere, splurge on how you do it. Buy a first-class seat. Have a limo pick you up. You decide. Whatever you choose, it's going to make the journey a destination in itself.

BUCKET LIST ENTRY #91

I'M GOING TO MAKE GETTING THERE BE ALL THE FUN BY:

BUCKET LIST ENTRY #92

Master a Dance

1. When I think of dancing, I think of: (check one)

   - ☐ *grace*
   - ☐ *poise*
   - ☐ *skills*
   - ☐ *being light on your feet*
   - ☐ *barfing*

2. Have you ever had any kind of dance classes or training?

   - ☐ *Yes*
   - ☐ *No*

3. Can you moonwalk? Whether yes or no, draw yourself moonwalking here.

4. If you've already had dance classes or training in one class, what's another dance you'd like to learn?

____

____

____

5. The Running Man is a more than respectable answer.

6. You prefer:

☐ *fast dancing*
☐ *slow dancing*
☐ *as-easy-to-learn-as-possible dancing*

7. Research a dance based on your answer above and go learn it. Take classes, learn from a friend, or even have our old grand tutorial friend in everything, the Internet, teach you.

BUCKET LIST ENTRY #92

I'M GOING TO BECOME DYNAMITE WITH THE DANCING BY:

____

____

____

____

____

BUCKET LIST ENTRY #93

Pull an All-Nighter—a Really Fun All-Nighter

1. If you had to stay up all night, how would you do it?

2. What things could you, if given the unlimited power of wakefulness, do all night long? List some here.

3. When was the last time you stayed up all night? Describe.

4. Was it for fun, or was it for un-fun (i.e., work)?

   ☐ *Fun!*
   ☐ *Not fun :(*

5. This time, it's going to be for fun. Think about a reason you'd want to stay up all night (read an entire book, take in a movie marathon, party and then go to the after-party, after-after party, and post-after-after party in which you wind up in someone's garage that doubles as a top-hat haberdashery). Put your answer down here, and make it happen 'til the sun comes up.

BUCKET LIST ENTRY #93

I'M GOING TO HAVE A LITERAL ALL-NIGHT-FUN-BLAST BY:

____

____

____

____

____

BUCKET LIST ENTRY #94

Take the Ultimate Themed Road Trip

1. List some of your previous road trips.

2. What was it that made these road trips memorable and/or awesome? Was it the destination? The theme? The company? All of the above?

3. Think about a particular themed road trip you've never done but would like to do and write it down here. Could you go see various baseball stadiums? Trek all the way down the West Coast? Visit every single doll and/or action-figure-themed museum in the southernmost states? Choose your theme, buckle up, and make it happen. And don't forget the industrial-sized cans of cheese balls.

BUCKET LIST ENTRY #94

I'm going to become the ultimate road warrior by going to:

(List all the destinations you will be stopping at here)

BUCKET LIST ENTRY #95

Express Your Feelings Publicly

1. Are you one of those people who wears your heart on your sleeve? Or is it more like tucked away in the glove box of your car, which is always in the garage with the garage door closed?

   ☐ *Emotional*
   ☐ *"Emotions? What emotions?"*

2. When it comes to feelings, what's the most daring thing you've ever done?

   ____

   ____

   ____

3. In this world, life is short. And more importantly, people tend to often shy away from telling others how they feel. So why not express yourself in a way you never have before? That is, *publicly.* Tell someone you love them in a crowded restaurant—loudly. Propose marriage on the JumboTron. Shout, *"I love this woman!"* from Seattle's Space Needle observation deck. Make your feelings a bombastic, big, honking, hairy deal for once. Regardless of what happens, you'll feel glad you did. Failed stadium screen marriage proposal notwithstanding.

BUCKET LIST ENTRY #95

I'm going to make the world my audience for a conversation with someone special by:

BUCKET LIST ENTRY #96

Dress Like Somebody Famous

1. Think of a famous person whose style you admire and write that person's name down here.

   ____

2. Do some research about where this person gets his or her clothes. Express your surprise, frustration, or disdain about how expensive the clothes are with an uncommonly used expression. ("Great Scott!" "Heavens to buckets!" and "Nomenclature!" are all good examples.)

3. Describe what that style is. Why do you gravitate toward it?

   ____

   ____

   ____

4. Circle what your "Here's how I wear it" stance would look like.

5. Since you presumably can't afford to look exactly like a famous person, match that person's look as best you can. Check out some thrift stores and online sales. See how well your celeb's look works for you. Who knows, you may have just found yourself a whole new style. Heavens to buckets, you look good!

BUCKET LIST ENTRY #96

I'M GOING TO WEAR IT BETTER BY:

BUCKET LIST ENTRY #97

Visit a Place of Uniquely Personal Historical Significance

1. Where were you born?

2. Your parents?

3. Your grandparents?

4. Write down some places you've visited that are historically significant to your family history. Have you been to the house your parents grew up in? Your sister's college apartment? Let us know in this space.

5. How far back can you trace your family history?

6. Going as far back as you can, find out where your earliest ancestors lived. Go there. Be as exact as possible. And get in touch with your roots.

BUCKET LIST ENTRY #97

I'M GOING TO SEARCH FOR MY FOREFATHERS' FOREFATHERS BY VISITING:

BUCKET LIST ENTRY #98

Tell an Epic Lie to a Stranger

1. What's the biggest lie you've ever told anyone?

2. What happened? Did you get found out? Explain your deceit and whether or not it led to any consequences.

3. If you could make something up about yourself—what you do for a living, who you're related to, the fact that you are the sole heir to the extensive Mister Salty pretzel fortune—what would it be? Write down your hypothetical truth-stretching here.

4. Practice your funny little lie or deceit, figure out how you can work it into conversation, and tell it to a stranger. Make sure the situation is innocuous enough to not cause damage or consequences to either party involved. Maybe it's the next time you're on an airplane, or in line with a sales clerk, or riding in a hot air balloon. You're so devious!

BUCKET LIST ENTRY #98

I'M GOING TO TELL A FRACTURED FAIRY TALE ABOUT MYSELF TO A STRANGER, WHICH IS THIS:

BUCKET LIST ENTRY #99

Destroy Something

1. Everyone should have the unforgettable experience of causing harmless destruction to a physical object. What's something you've always day-dreamed about destroying? Is it that printer that doesn't print? Your old rickety fence? Your high-school Nova that sounds and smells like a sweaty rubber foundry?

____

____

____

____

2. Now that you've identified the object, identify the best and/or most pleasurable way you could destroy and dispose of it. Via sledgehammer? Via regular hammer? Via Arm & Hammer? After this step, just wait. And when it comes time to replace said object, send it off in style by annihilating it with your own hands.

____

____

____

____

____

3. As a bonus, come up with an epic sound you will make when you destroy the hated object. "Boom!" "Crushfest!" or "Ricky Rickshaw!" are all good examples. Write it down here so you'll commit to it:

BUCKET LIST ENTRY #99

Boom! I'm going to enjoy watching the physical deterioration of something at my hand by:

BUCKET LIST ENTRY #100

Witness One of Nature's Most Rarely Occurring Events

1. What would you say is the most rare event you've ever witnessed in your life?

2. Why was it so special?

3. How likely are you to see it again? Pick the best answer below:

- ☐ *as likely as you are to hear the phrase "What a gas!" make a comeback*
- ☐ *as likely as Roadrunner is to make Wile E. Coyote his right-hand man in a competitive paintball game*
- ☐ *as likely as you are to see Sasquatch in his habitat for a second time*

4. What's one thing you've always wanted to see happen in nature but never have (and fear that you never will)? If you need some ideas, feel free to research natural events.

5. Seek it out. Mark it on your calendar. Stalk it. See it. Change your life.

BUCKET LIST ENTRY #100

I'M GOING TO WITNESS THE MOTHER OF ALL MOTHER NATURE OCCURRENCES BY:

BUCKET LIST ENTRY #101

Become a Bar Sport Champion

1. Which of these either describes you or sounds most appealing?

   - ☐ *Pool shark*
   - ☐ *Dart ace*
   - ☐ *Bowling baron/baroness*
   - ☐ *Beanbag-tossing tool of God*
   - ☐ *Quidditch Quail of Hope*
   - ☐ *Euchre Eucharist*
   - ☐ *Ping-Pong pinpoint control wizard*
   - ☐ *Kobayashi Kobayashi*

2. Could you actually see yourself as some sort of Quail of Hope? If so, prove it by getting "Quail" tattooed along one set of knuckles and "of Hope" tattooed on the other (squeeze it in to make room).

3. Are you already a grand master champion at any of the above activities?

   - ☐ *Yes*
   - ☐ *No*

4. If so, what type of grand championship could you enter to prove your grand champion status? City? County? State? National? Transcontinental?

   And if not: Do everything you can to become a grand master champion at one of the above leisure sporty pursuits. Hone your craft. Challenge all comers. Commit for a period of time (six months minimum), and see just how good you can get.

BUCKET LIST ENTRY #101

I'm going to become a leisure sport medalist by:

____

____

____

____

____

BUCKET LIST ENTRY #102

Become One with Winter

1. When it's wintertime, how cold does it get where you live?

   ☐ *Cooler than a polar bear's toenails*
   ☐ *A little chilly, but nothing a chili dog can't fix*
   ☐ *"Sssssssssssssssssssssss" (the sound of someone trying to talk through lips so chapped from cold weather that words are no longer possible)*
   ☐ *In wintertime, I can still wear those pants that are also shorts and sometimes even unzip the pants part and hang out just fine*
   ☐ *Moderately Hades*

2. What's your favorite wintertime activity?

___

___

___

3. Does your favorite wintertime activity involve embracing the winter weather, or is it more like pushing away Chinese food you didn't actually order and you aren't even hungry for?

   - ☐ *Embrace*
   - ☐ *Chinese food when full*

4. If you're an embracer, think about something new you could try that could push your embracing into a new winter hug you've never had. Maybe a polar bear plunge? Skiing the Swiss Alps? Some sort of winter-coat modeling career? Think about it.

   ____

   ____

   ____

5. When it comes to winter, if you're a pusher-awayer, a naysayer, a total wintertime player hater, it's time to suck it up and try something new. That is, do something unique this winter. This should come easier for you than you may think, due to the fact that your winter experiences are most likely minimal and therefore an open, friendly, ice-coated book of goodness in which to explore.

BUCKET LIST ENTRY #102

I'M GOING TO TURN THE COLDNESS OF WINTER INTO A HEARTWARMING GOOD TIME BY:

____

____

____

____

____

BUCKET LIST ENTRY #103

Develop a Go-To Magic Trick

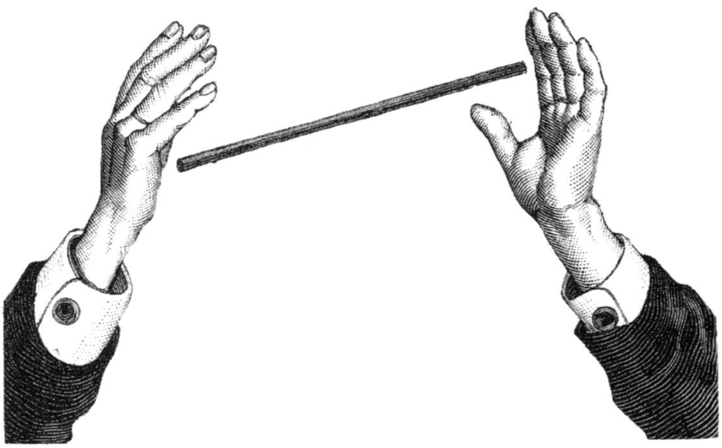

1. Could you, right now, pull rolled one-hundred dollar bills out of the nose of the stranger nearest you?

   ☐ *Yes*
   ☐ *No*

2. Could you, right now, pull a rabbit not just from your hat but from your Ugg boot?

   ☐ *Yes*
   ☐ *No*

3. Could you, right now, get your Subway sandwich cooked the exact way you order it in less than four minutes—even factoring in that you asked for the bread toasted and will have to deal with a few questions or asides about how "it's going to burn, for sure"?

   ☐ *Yes*
   ☐ *No*

4. If you answered yes to any of the above, you are already a magician. What this means is that you already must surely have a go-to magic trick. Write it down here and be done.

   ____

   ____

5. If not, well then, let's rub our hands together, shout, "Rugendo!" and by golly, get down to business! What do you want to do?

- ☐ *Saw somebody in half*
- ☐ *Perform a card trick*
- ☐ *Pull something (quarter, rabbit, fedora) from something*
- ☐ *Other*

6. Figure out how to learn one of the above and perfect it. Boom, you're an instant party hit. *Boom!* Dollars to donuts, a card trick is easiest to learn. But if you're feeling especially godlike, see if you can be one of the few lucky ones that can get a magician in the know to reveal his secret and learn his trick. Either that or get the answers from elsewhere. Magic!

BUCKET LIST ENTRY #103

I'M GOING TO FIND SOME POCUS TO GO WITH MY AMBITION FOR HOCUS BY:

____

____

____

____

____

BUCKET LIST ENTRY #104

Make Up Your Very Own Superhero Persona

1. Everyone needs his or her own superhero persona. Pick the single superpower you wish you could have and write it here.

2. Good. Now pick some aspect of your own life that you could make uniquely yours. Are you a fast runner? Are you great at filing? Do you have a third nostril? Pick a talent.

3. Awesome. Now pick a name that works with that talent. Here are some notable examples, all of which you are free to use:

    a. *Earnest Man*
    b. *Dashiki Dash*
    c. *Nostril Boy, son of Much Mucus*
    d. *Lord of the Files*
    e. *Roscoe P. Coldchain*
    f. *Alexis*

4. Great. Now list the accessories you want.

5. Splendid. Now, as you start to see this superhero persona take shape before your soon-to-be-superhero eyes (even without X-ray vision), draw yourself as a superhero, complete with your superhero moniker at the top. That sound you hear is a group of citizens rejoicing! Also, overall crime trembling. And a stray cat crying.

BUCKET LIST ENTRY #104

I AM NOW MY OWN SUPERHERO, AND THIS IS WHAT I LOOK LIKE:

BUCKET LIST ENTRY #105

Become a Connoisseur of a Particular Food

1. What food interests you enough that you'd be willing to write a mushy open love letter to it, pretending it's your one and only true love for whom you'd go to war with, even if it meant cheating to pass a physical?

 ____

 ____

 ____

2. Write down any fun factoids you might have about this food.

 ____

 ____

 ____

3. Are you factoid devoid? (Meaning no, you do not have much in the way of facts.)

 ☐ *Yes*
 ☐ *No*

4. Are you factoid deployed? (Meaning yes, you have many facts.)

   ☐ *Yes*
   ☐ *No*

5. Are you annoyed?

   ☐ *Yes*
   ☐ *No*

6. To become a connoisseur, you must become thoroughly educated, to the point where your taste buds dance differently to many seemingly imperceptible but individual flavors. Also, you may have to start wearing a monocle. Are you willing to wear a monocle?

   ☐ *Yes*
   ☐ *No*

7. Now that that's settled, gather delicious knowledge and teach others so that they too may know the culinary delights that are known to dance their way through your stomach's heart.

BUCKET LIST ENTRY #105

MONOCLE OR NOT, I'M GOING TO TURN MY FOOD LOVE INTO FOOD-OVERLY-AMOROUS-EMBRACE BY BECOMING A CONNOISSEUR OF:

____

____

____

____

____

BUCKET LIST ENTRY #106

Make a Dramatic Change to Your Appearance

1. What would you, if you could, change about your physical appearance?

___

___

___

2. Would it require surgery to do so?

☐ *Yes*
☐ *No*

3. If no, list some ways you could change what you want to change. If yes, pick a different answer—we're not trying to talk you into something that heavy. We're speaking on purely exploratory terms here.

___

___

___

4. Would this change involve swapping out your old acid-washed jeans for some Z. Cavariccis?

   - ☐ *Yes*
   - ☐ *No*

5. Would it involve trading your eyebrows for eyebrows that each resemble the Nike swoosh?

   - ☐ *Yes*
   - ☐ *No*

6. Would it involve you, as Nicolas Cage, trading your face with that of John Travolta?

   - ☐ *Yes*
   - ☐ *No*

7. If you answered yes to any of the previous three inquiries, congratulations—your job is done here. If not, look at your list from Question 3 and pick one. Are you game for a dramatic makeover? A fresh hair color? A complete wardrobe changeup? Commit to it—and let your new self shine.

BUCKET LIST ENTRY #106

I'M GOING TO CHANGE MY LOOK BY:

____

____

____

____

____

BUCKET LIST ENTRY #107

Give Your Home That Extra Touch You've Always Dreamed Of

1. Answer this. To you, a home is a person's:

   - ☐ *castle*
   - ☐ *ahhhhhhhhh palace*
   - ☐ *chill spot*

2. Assuming you take at least some level of pleasure from being at home (regardless of where that home is or what it consists of), describe what features that ideal home would contain but currently does not. A waterbed? A gazebo? A wet bar with a robot bartender? You call it.

___

___

___

3. Where would you put said home addition? Describe.

4. Can your will match your ambitions? Is this a project you would ever conceivably take on? Or at the very least, pay for to make happen? If so, do it. If not, what's something else you can do to give your home that extra touch you've always been waiting for? Is it a piece of art? Knocking down a wall? Replacing a window so you can finally get some air in there? Figure it out and make it happen.

BUCKET LIST ENTRY #107

I'M GOING TO PROVE HOME IS WHERE THE HEART IS BY GIVING MYSELF A NICE LITTLE UPGRADE IN THE FORM OF:

BUCKET LIST ENTRY #108

START YOUR OWN BUSINESS

1. Have you ever had the dream of leaving it all behind and going out on your own?

   ☐ *Yes*
   ☐ *No*

2. Are you then shaken back to reality by your sizable number of monetary responsibilities and commitments, including, but not limited to, children and dog?

   ☐ *Yes*
   ☐ *No*

3. Are you already on your own, scaling the high seas of entrepreneurial dream-dom, plowing ahead, living the life?

   ☐ *Yes*
   ☐ *No*

4. If you answered yes, are you happy with it? Has it been worth it? If it really hasn't, maybe now is the right time to consider something else—maybe a different venture for yourself. And if you're not on your own yet, maybe now is the time to try it. Seriously. If money and responsibility were not a concern, what would be your dream entrepreneurial business effort? Opening your own bar? Your own store with your own shabby chic line of purse liners? Your own coffee shop in which you call everybody "hon"? Dream big.

5. Okay, now that you're swelled with ambition, come up with a slogan for your business. It doesn't have to be customer facing. But doing so can help frame up what your business philosophy is. Plus, it's fun. After all, who doesn't like to think of slogans? Note: "Be all you can be" is already taken. Also, "It is what it is" is not an acceptable business slogan.

6. All right, then. You've got your slogan; you've got your idea. You're good to go.

BUCKET LIST ENTRY #108

I'm going to ride the wave of my entrepreneurial aspirations by:

BUCKET LIST ENTRY #109

Get Famous

1. Think about how famous John Tesh is.

2. Do you think it's possible to become even more famous than John Tesh?[1]

   ☐ *Yes*
   ☐ *No*

3. How could you, based on the skills and life experience you have, make yourself into a famously well-known big deal? If you're a writer, could you write a bestseller? If you're fashion-forward, could you work your way up to the cover of *Glamour*? Could you run for and win political office?

[1] *Note*: Void if you're John Tesh.

4. Let's be real. A lot of hitting it big comes from hard work. A lot of it comes from luck, too. But you never know. And just being a part of the process would be fun, even if you only give it a go for a little while before packing it in and realizing that measuring up to Tesh just isn't possible. So just by trying, you'll get an A for effort, regardless. But just for fun, paste a small picture on this fake cover of *Time* magazine, just to see how it would look.

BUCKET LIST ENTRY #109

I'm going to become more famous than John Tesh by:

BUCKET LIST ENTRY #110

Do Something That Totally Transcends Your Current Age

1. How old are you?

2. How old are you in marmoset years? (That would be your age plus 9, minus 7, times 8, carry the 1. Not really.)

3. If you're over forty, name some things you liked to do when you were in your twenties. If you're under forty, name some things you'll want to do when you're fifty-five. Some examples: concerts, road trip to Graceland, play shuffleboard on a cruise ship, get a tattoo, and so on.

4. Pick which one of these sounds the most fun to you. If you're older, could you still do it now? If you're younger, same question. Is it possible? If not, pick something else and watch the fascinating case study of you being totally out of your element unfold.

BUCKET LIST ENTRY #110

I'M GOING TO BECOME AN AGELESS WONDER BY:

BUCKET LIST ENTRY #111

Get on a Reality Show

1. What special talents do you have?

____

____

____

2. How much do you think the world as a whole would benefit from seeing those talents in action:

   a. *It wouldn't change the world*
   b. *It wouldn't be groundbreaking, but it would still be entertaining to the world*
   c. *A new world would have to be created after the result of seeing my talents in action*
   d. *He's got the whole world in his hand*

3. What are your favorite reality shows?

   ☐ *Shows about comedy*
   ☐ *Shows about physical challenges*
   ☐ *Shows about music*
   ☐ *Shows about partying*
   ☐ *Other*

4. List any specific favorite reality shows you have. If you don't have any, that's okay. We know reality shows can be polarizing. So instead, do this: research the existing reality shows that are out there, and, whether you hate them or not, match up the closest one you can find to one of your special talents. Then, try out! You might just become the next reality show superstar.

BUCKET LIST ENTRY #111

I'M GOING TO PLUNGE HEADFIRST INTO THE WORLD OF REALITY TELEVISION BY:

Index

FINIS

About the Author

Andrew Gall is a writer of both books and advertising. His first book, a great ape caper of ridiculousness titled *Everything Is Better with a Gorilla*, was published in 2010. He lives in Chicago with his wife, Megan.

About the Designer

Matt Webb is an art director and designer originally from Colorado. For the past seven years he has worked on advertising campaigns for many major companies. Matt has recently started working independently, freelancing for advertising agencies and developing designed objects of his own. He lives in Chicago with his girlfriend, Jenny, and their dog, Lucy.

Art Credits

Table © 1962 Dover Publications Inc.
Boats © 1962 Dover Publications Inc.
Revolver © 2001 Dover Publications Inc.
Banana © iStockphoto.com/Bellott
Lick © Jupiterimages Corporation
Rainbow by Matt Webb
Swim © 1962 Dover Publications Inc.
Birch © 1962 Dover Publications Inc.
Swing by Matt Webb
Lemurs © 1962 Dover Publications Inc.
Writer by Matt Webb
Clown © Jupiterimages Corporation
Pinhead by Matt Webb
Squirrel © 1962 Dover Publications Inc.
Gladiator © 1980 Dover Publications Inc.
Car © 2001 Dover Publications Inc.
USA Maps by Matt Webb
Invention © 1994 Dover Publications Inc.
Man © 1983 Dover Publications Inc.
Horse © Jupiterimages Corporation
Nuns by Matt Webb
Jump Rope © 1982 Dover Publications Inc.
Neptune © 1987 Dover Publications Inc.
Knight © 1978 Dover Publications Inc.
Baseball © Jupiterimages Corporation
Hippie by Matt Webb
Dinosaur © Jupiterimages Corporation
Tightrope © 1982 Dover Publications Inc.
Jockey © 1987 Dover Publications Inc.
Top Hat © 1980 Dover Publications Inc.
Devils © 1962 Dover Publications Inc.
Monsters © 1962, 1998 Dover Publications Inc.
Reader © Jupiterimages Corporation
Cave © Jupiterimages Corporation
Drummer © Jupiterimages Corporation
Dog by Matt Webb
Waterfall © Jupiterimages Corporation
Loom © Jupiterimages Corporation
Museum © Jupiterimages Corporation
Carnival © Jupiterimages Corporation
Men © Jupiterimages Corporation
Handshake © Jupiterimages Corporation
Spoons © 2006 Dover Publications Inc.
Model © Jupiterimages Corporation
Authors © Jupiterimages Corporation
Ringmaster © Jupiterimages Corporation
Musician © Jupiterimages Corporation
Rock by Matt Webb
Speech by Matt Webb
Fright © Jupiterimages Corporation
Number Line by Matt Webb
Theme Park © Jupiterimages Corporation
Fashion © 1980 Dover Publications Inc.
Graduate © 1980 Dover Publications Inc.
Donkeys © Jupiterimages Corporation
Gorillas © Jupiterimages Corporation
Badgers © Jupiterimages Corporation
Home © Jupiterimages Corporation
Spiritual © 1980 Dover Publications Inc.
W by Matt Webb
Swoosh rendered by Matt Webb
Peace sign by Matt Webb
Famous © 1998 Dover Publications Inc.
Event © 1982 Dover Publications Inc.
Food © 1983 Dover Publications Inc.
Holidays © Jupiterimages Corporation
Gathering © Jupiterimages Corporation
Native © 1987 Dover Publications Inc.
Party © 1983 Dover Publications Inc.
Unicorn © 1998 Dover Publications Inc.
Potato by Matt Webb
Feast © 1983 Dover Publications Inc.
Baby © Jupiterimages Corporation
Trip © Jupiterimages Corporation
Animal Party © Jupiterimages Corporation
Nature © Jupiterimages Corporation
Blackboard © Jupiterimages Corporation
Technology © 1980 Dover Publications Inc.
No by Matt Webb
Auction © 1990 Dover Publications Inc.
Inhibitions © 1982 Dover Publications Inc.
Ladder © Jupiterimages Corporation
Bar © Jupiterimages Corporation
Masks #1 and #2 © Jupiterimages Corporation
Mask #3 © 2011 Dover Publications Inc.
Romance ©1982 Dover Publications Inc.
Emcee © Jupiterimages Corporation
Dinner © 1983 Dover Publications Inc.
Disks by Matt Webb
Job © Jupiterimages Corporation
Camera © Jupiterimages Corporation
Outdoors © 2001 Dover Publications Inc.
Ad © Jupiterimages Corporation
Gymnast © Jupiterimages Corporation
Bicycles by Matt Webb
Horse © 2001 Dover Publications Inc.
Money © Jupiterimages Corporation
Train © 1987 Dover Publications Inc.
Pamper © Jupiterimages Corporation
Indulgence by Matt Webb
Cocktail © 1983 Dover Publications Inc.
Chef © 1990 Dover Publications Inc.
Scale © Jupiterimages Corporation
Tradition © 1987 Dover Publications Inc.
Expert © 1987 Dover Publications Inc.
Getaway © Jupiterimages Corporation
Movie © Jupiterimages Corporation
Country © Jupiterimages Corporation
Flags © Jupiterimages Corporation
Spectacles © 2001 Dover Publications Inc.
Man © Jupiterimages Corporation
Road Trip © 2011 Dover Publications Inc.
Furniture © 1980 Dover Publications Inc.
Music © 1980 Dover Publications Inc.
Letter © 1990 Dover Publications Inc.
Spy © 2011 Dover Publications Inc.
History © Jupiterimages Corporation
Television by Matt Webb
Travel © 2011 Dover Publications Inc.
Dance © Jupiterimages Corporation
All-nighter © Jupiterimages Corporation
Road Trip © Jupiterimages Corporatio
Feelings © 1982 Dover Publications In
Dress © Jupiterimages Corporation
Stances © Jupiterimages Corporation
Location © Jupiterimages Corporatio
Stranger © Jupiterimages Corporation
Balloon © Jupiterimages Corporation
Volcano © Jupiterimages Corporation
Pool © Jupiterimages Corporation
Winter © 1980 Dover Publications Inc
Magic © Jupiterimages Corporation
Super Hero © 1982 Dover Publications Inc.
Eat © 1983 Dover Publications Inc.
Wolf © Jupiterimages Corporation
Dream Home © 1990 Dover Publications Inc.
Business © 1990 Dover Publications I
Famous © Jupiterimages Corporation
Magazine by Matt Webb
Sled by Matt Webb
Reality by Matt Webb
Grave © 1962 Dover Publications Inc.